rebuilding

confirmation

rebuilding
confirmation

BECAUSE WE NEED
MORE THAN ANOTHER GRADUATION

Christopher Wesley

Ave Maria Press AVE Notre Dame, Indiana

Founded in 1865, Ave Maria Press is a ministry of the United States Province of Holy Cross.

www.avemariapress.com

Paperback: ISBN-13 978-1-59471-585-3

E-book: ISBN-13 978-1-59471-586-0

Cover and text design by Katherine J. Ross.

Printed and bound in the United States of America.

Library of Congress Cataloging-in-Publication Data is available.

This book is dedicated to the men and women,
especially my mother,
who took time to share with me their love for the Lord.
Thank you for showing me
that the greatest relationship any person can have
is with God.

CONTENTS

PREFACE

Why Does This Matter?

On the very last day of high school I ran to my car, popped in the CD, and blared Alice Cooper's 1970s hit song "School's Out" across the parking lot. I shouted along: "No more pencils! No more books! No more teachers' dirty looks!" I was done; college was going to be different—or at least that's what I thought.

The emotions that I had leaving school that day were similar to the ones I felt after my Confirmation Mass. I was so happy to have no more religious education, no more workbooks, and no more memorize *this* and memorize *that*. I was done! Now, don't get me wrong, I still planned on going to Mass and I loved my youth group. But I was done with the whole formation thing. The idea of having to go back into a classroom after hours in school and grinding through a dense Confirmation workbook made me queasy.

I'm willing to bet that I'm not the only one who had those emotions. For a lot of teens, getting confirmed means no more religious education, no more sacrificing a weeknight to some pretty dry presentation of Catholicism, and, for too many, it means no more going to Mass on Sundays.

And it's not just the teens that are rejoicing when it's all over. It's the parents who don't have to drag their teens to another activity. It's the youth ministers or directors of religious education (DRE) who are relieved that they survived another season of reluctant participation. Everyone seems happy to get it over with, which if you think about it is odd.

I don't claim to be a biblical scholar, but I've never seen the part of the Bible where Jesus says, "Congratulations! You're a disciple now!" In fact it's quite the opposite. Jesus is constantly telling us to keep *going*! So, if that's the vision he has for us in our faith journey, shouldn't we see Confirmation a little differently? Instead of seeing it as an end to something painful, we should look at it as the beginning of something amazing. It is after all a sacrament of initiation. It helps us *begin* a new season of our discipleship, rather than end our years of religious formation.

You are probably reading this book because there is something about Confirmation preparation that bothers you. Maybe it bothers you because you are tired of people just going through the motions. If you are a DRE or youth minister, it may feel as if every year you have to drag parents and teens through the mud just to get them to show up. If you are parent, Confirmation prep likely bothers you because you look at what your church provides for content and wonder, *Is this enough?*

Confirmation preparation probably also bothers you because somehow the process in most parishes has been made overly complicated. It's no longer user friendly because of the rules, requirements, and regulations. DREs can't easily reach the next generation because going through preparation is more complicated than getting a mortgage. Parents and teens often struggle to find value in many of the required activities in the process.

All of this bothers you because you love the sacraments and the church. Confirmation is a beautiful expression of faith that carries a lot of meaning. If you pick up the book of Acts and read about the Pentecost event, you likely wonder, Is that sort of powerful experience of the Holy Spirit even remotely possible now?

The answer is yes! The answer is that Confirmation preparation in the local parish can be saved. It can be so much more than just another checklist or series of hoops to jump through. My hope is that as you read this book, you'll be encouraged to lean into the tension that Confirmation preparation can bring. I'll share with you what we've done at my parish, Church of the Nativity, in Timonium, Maryland, to move a process that was once painful into something teens are excited about even before they get started. We celebrate Confirmation with high school students, but most of what I offer here will easily transfer to middle school students, and much of it—especially the information about systemic solutions—will also work in parishes that practice the restored order of initiation where children are confirmed at the same time they receive First Communion.

We don't have everything figured out when it comes to Confirmation, but we've seen a lot of progress at Church of the Nativity. Fewer teens are leaving, and increasing numbers of them are getting involved and stepping up as leaders in our parish. This book is the story of what we've learned, what we are doing, and where we hope to go.

If you are a parent, DRE or faith-formation director, youth minister, deacon, pastoral life director, or pastor, I hope this book will be a tool that you bring to the parish staff and let it help you answer the question, *What is Confirmation going to look like in our parish?*

Part I
EMBRACING THE OPPORTUNITY

1
OWN THE SITUATION

The rest of that generation were also gathered to their ancestors, and a later generation arose that did not know the Lord or the work he had done for Israel.

—Judges 2:10

Who's to blame when it comes to failing Confirmation prep programs? Everyone has his or her own opinion. And while we can play the blame game, the real question should be, Who owns the problem? Because when you own the problem you take the first step toward finding a solution.

One night as I was setting up for our high school program, our pastor stopped by to see how everything was going. I was in the middle of making copies of our small-group questions for our leaders and feeling a little stressed out. I didn't want to let on that I was feeling overwhelmed, so I replied, "It's all good, just a little busy work before the students get here."

He smiled and responded, "Oh, good. By the way did you know that one of the new couches that you recently bought is broken?"

I wanted to ignore what he had just said; there was a lot I had to get done. But those couches had been the source of a good bit of tension. I had spent months researching and comparing prices, and hours explaining and pleading with leadership why our ministry needed those couches to grow disciples. In the end I had won the battle in proving why this investment in youth ministry was so important. It took me a year to earn the right to have those couches, and now one of them was broken!

Something inside of me snapped. I couldn't ignore it any longer, so I walked out into the hallway where our students congregate.

There it was as clear as day. It was as if someone had decided that the $400 couch from IKEA would make a great trampoline.

My frustration grew to anger. If I had the strength of the Hulk, I would have picked up that couch and thrown it across the hall. I vowed vengeance and set off to find the responsible party. That's when the IKEA couch witch hunt began. Fortunately, there were not a lot of people in the building, so finding a guilty party should have been easy. It was not.

I quickly removed the pastor from my list of suspects; there was no chance he was responsible. I concluded that none of my adult volunteers would have committed such a crime without confessing. I went to Chris, our student worship bandleader, who was coordinating a practice. I asked him for an account of all student band members. They all had alibis.

I started wandering around asking anyone who was in the building about that couch. I needed someone to blame. I was confused, anxious, and angry. And I was avoiding the one thing I should have been concerned with: fixing the problem. I had a broken couch that needed to be removed, and instead of getting it out of people's way I felt driven to find someone to blame.

FINDING THE PROBLEM

Finding out who is responsible for the woes of Confirmation preparation is a witch hunt. In the end all you do is make yourself more angry and frustrated. When it comes to fixing the problem we tend to dwell too much on who's responsible for the problem and not enough on exploring who is responsible for the solution. Not only do we look for someone to blame, but also we buy into a few myths that perpetuate the lengthy search.

Myth 1: Teenagers Just Don't Care
When teenagers don't meet the requirements or don't show up, we tend to believe that they just don't care. It's easy to accuse teenagers of being apathetic when it comes to their faith. After all, it appears

as if they are too immersed in the material world and their own particular activities and social connections to really focus on Christ. We tend to see teenagers as self-centered, immature, and driven to engage in events only when it seems everyone else is, or at least when the cool crowd is involved.

The reality is that teenagers do care about the spiritual life. Regardless of the topic, the question they ask is, "Why does it matter?" The problem is that we often tell them what they need to do to "get" confirmed without taking the time to explain why Confirmation matters, why church matters, and why having a relationship with Jesus Christ matters.

As youth ministers, catechists, and directors of religious education (DREs), we need to clarify the purpose of Confirmation, first in our own minds and then with those we invite to the sacrament. We need to take the time to explain why it matters in the lives of our young people. When you can answer that big question for them, then you can expect a return on your hard work and your investment in the process and in their lives.

Myth 2: The Parents Have Given Up

It's easy to blame parents and resign ourselves to the myth that they have given up. We often believe they let their teens walk all over them and that the only reason parents are doing this whole Confirmation thing is so that their parents will back off. We all find it easy to believe (and complain) that parents are more concerned with getting their teen into a good college than helping them get to know Jesus.

The truth is that parents need assistance. While they are primarily responsible for the faith formation of their teens, there isn't any clear manual to help them do that. In fact there is often precious little real support for them in our parishes. If you are coordinating your Confirmation preparation, you need to make sure that parents know they aren't alone. Don't just supply resources; instead, be a resource they can go to when their teens will not talk to them.

Myth 3: The Director of
Religious Education Is a Control Freak

Some of us believe that all our parish DRE wants is control and that he or she doesn't care about really helping teens understand. We think the DRE is a school-principal wannabe, wanting to be "the boss" rather than a partner. We think to ourselves, *Maybe if she watched a little television she would know what's going on in the world.*

Most DREs have a lot on their plate. On top of regular religious education, we might be asking them to take on much more. It's crucial that parishes find these ministers support and eventually appoint someone (paid or volunteer) who will focus solely on sacramental preparation.

Myth 4: The Youth Minister Is Reckless

This myth holds that youth ministers really only care about being a friend to the youth of the parish. Being their friend makes them feel good, important, and as if they have a place in the parish and the world. We think all they know is games, what toppings on pizza taste good, and how to throw a Frisbee. Youth ministers are more of event and activities planners than people responsible enough to lead the next generation. How do they even stay employed?

Like the DRE, youth ministers' plates are often too full with a variety of responsibilities outside of their core job description. Plus, youth ministers get into ministry to be relational. If your Confirmation program is not relational, you are creating a competing and broken system. Give your youth minister guidance and crucial support.

Myth 5: The Pastor Doesn't
Want Anything to Do with the Process

Does he even care about teenagers? The only time he talks about them is to complain. He's constantly slashing the budget and never shows up to any of the classes.

The pastor does care, but he might not know how to comfortably approach teens. Instead of resenting him for not being more hands on, invite him to be a part of the planning and vision casting. Think about helping him take small steps toward not just understanding teens but also coming to value their role in the parish. Help your teens get to know him and come to value his role.

While these myths focus on different people, what they have in common is that they are focused on *people*. Too often we place blame on people, when the problem really has to do with *systems*. The reason Confirmation preparation hasn't been working isn't because of a reckless generation or disenfranchised parish staff. It's because what worked half a century ago is no longer effective today. Just like the world around it, preparation needs to change.

If you are going to change anything you need to start looking at the systems that feed and fuel the problem. If you are dissatisfied with your Confirmation program, start looking at the systems that impact and influence it. Here are a few of the systems problems we identified as we began to rebuild our program.

System Issue 1: An Unclear Purpose

If you want someone to commit time and energy to something, you need to answer the question, Why does this matter? Knowing exactly why receiving the sacrament matters is key to having teens, parents, and the church community embrace the journey.

The *Catechism of the Catholic Church* (*CCC*) tells us that Confirmation brings an increase and deepening of baptismal grace:

- it roots us more deeply in the divine filiation which makes us cry, "Abba! Father!";
- it unites us more firmly to Christ;
- it increases the gifts of the Holy Spirit in us;
- it renders our bond with the Church more perfect; [and]
- it gives us a special strength of the Holy Spirit to spread and defend the faith by word and action as true witnesses of Christ, to confess the name of Christ boldly, and never to be ashamed of the Cross.

—*Catechism of the Catholic Church*, 1303

If you've grown up in the church and have a deep understanding of the sacrament, what the *Catechism* teaches is so moving. The problem is that people who are less engaged than you and I want to know what this will look like in their everyday life. Preparing your students for Confirmation is all about answering the question, *Why does this matter?*

Answering that question is not simple. Right now teens are hearing a lot of messages about what should matter in their lives. They are told that grades, scholarships, trophies, and other résumé builders are what will lead them to a fuller life. You and I know the only message that's true is the one from Jesus when he taught, "I came so that they might have life and have it more abundantly" (Jn 10:10).

Confirmation unites us more firmly with Christ, and that's what brings us a full life. You and I are responsible for clarifying with teens why this part of their journey is so important. Instead of teaching them only (or even mostly) *what* they need to know, we need tell our teenagers that Confirmation preparation is for learning the next steps that will lead to a better you.

That's it. Preparing for Confirmation is learning how to be a disciple of Christ, because we believe that's the path to a fuller and more fulfilling life. Give them a purpose and watch them dive in.

System Issue 2: More Schooling

Teens spend a great deal of their waking hours in school for most of each year. Nothing sounds less attractive to them than more school. To make Confirmation prep even less appealing is that this schooling takes place in the evening, when they are tired and easily resentful of their free time or homework or money-earning time being chewed up by a program they don't really see a value in.

Confirmation textbooks, homework, and testing are only going to lead to frustration and resentment. Plus, if you think about it, how much can you teach in a Confirmation prep course? You might have them for two hours per week over the span of twelve weeks.

That's trying to cram over two thousand years of church history, doctrine, theology, and practice into about twenty-four hours.

The problem with setting up Confirmation preparation like a formal classroom is that you are adding to the constant noise of information overload that teenagers face on a regular basis. In later chapters we'll discuss content in some detail, but the solution to the system problem is twofold.

The first part is that Confirmation preparation needs to be relational. If you are going to break open deep, enriching information with teens, they need to do that with someone they trust. To build that trust you need to find people who are focused on building relationships. You need people who want to meet the candidates where they are in their faith journeys and help them take a next step toward a deeper relationship with Jesus Christ.

The second part is narrowing your focus and teaching less for a greater impact. In other words, ask yourself what is essential for candidates to know that will help them continue growing in discipleship after they are confirmed.

The list of topics, tools, habits, and facts that we want to communicate to our young people seems to be endless. It is certainly daunting! The truth is that with the limited time you and I have with them, we have to focus on a few important truths that will have significant impact. In his book *7 Practices of Effective Ministry*, Andy Stanley writes, "If you are responsible for training in your organization you must learn to prioritize information. You have to take a look at what your target audience needs to know and separate what is most important from what is just interesting" (122).

A classroom is all about getting the information communicated, but when you set up your sacramental prep to be relational, it's about investing in your vision, your hope of who the candidate will become.

System Issue 3: No Teamwork

It doesn't matter who is charged with leading the Confirmation program. In the end it's a parish-wide responsibility. What that means is that the pastor, DRE, youth minister, and everyone else involved needs to join hands and get on board—together.

I'm willing to bet most people feel this way, but when they try to get others to buy in, all they get are empty promises. And while you can't control others, you can influence their buy-in.

The buy-in comes with you presenting the right vision. The buy-in comes from putting others before you. The buy-in comes from being able to communicate that without fully confirmed disciples of Jesus Christ, the Church will falter and eventually cease to be.

If you look at the biblical story of Joshua, you'll discover a man who had faith that God was with him. You'll see someone who had courage. However, you'll also discover his inability to help the next generation come to the Lord.

> The rest of that generation were also gathered to their ancestors, and a later generation arose that did not know the LORD or the work he had done for Israel.
>
> —Judges 2:10

How could that happen? It's because no one took the time to share with the next generation what it looked like to have a relationship with God.

It's time to stop playing the blame game. It's time to look at our next generation of Catholic disciples as an investment that can bear fruit and have a greater impact on the Church and in the world than we can ever imagine. Confirmation preparation might seem like a thorn in your side. It might feel like one of those impossible tasks. But it's worth it; you just need to own the challenge, own the situation, find solutions, and trust God.

2
MAKE IT MORE THAN GRADUATION

The way of loyalty I have chosen;
I have kept your judgments.
I cling to your testimonies, LORD;
do not let me come to shame.
I will run the way of your commandments,
for you will broaden my heart.

—Psalm 119:30–32

When it comes to Confirmation, the end result is treated a lot like a graduation. The first question I get when parents and teens start asking about the program late each summer is, When is the Confirmation Mass? And I get it because people want to invite family and friends from out of town. They want to celebrate this accomplishment of completing faith formation. But you and I know that Confirmation is more than a graduation.

There is a paradigm shift that needs to happen in order for Confirmation prep to regain purpose and value. That comes from having clarity of vision. If the vision is clear it becomes more than a graduation from religious education. It becomes something more than anyone can imagine. We just need to treat it as something more.

THEY DON'T HAVE TO DO THIS

Every year at the first information meeting parents freak out when I say to their teenagers, "You don't have to do this." In their mind

I'm the one person they are counting on to take their side. I'm the person that is going to convince their teenagers that they need to do this. For a lot of parents this feels like their last shot at giving their kids any type of faith formation and with a few brief words I seem to have blown it!

I would love to come through for parents on these expectations, but the reality is that's not always possible. Each candidate has a choice, and that's why we say, "You don't have to do this." It's a reminder that they have free will and are in control of the next step.

When you tell people that they don't have to do something it removes a burden. You are telling them that this is a choice and they control the decision. When you empower the candidates, they'll respond with openness to what you have to offer. That's why we also tell them, "You get to do this."

Going from *you have* to *you get* is bigger than just swapping out one word. It's the changing of a paradigm. It not only puts the control back in the hands of the candidates but also helps shape their recognition that they have a right and a responsibility to choose the next step in their relationships with Christ.

The question you and I need to answer for them is what do they *get* by participating in the preparation. In sports you get a trophy. In school you get a diploma. In every other club, class, and activity there is some tangible reward for their efforts.

You and I know that what a person receives from the sacraments is more than anything the world could ever offer. In fact it's the beginning of something huge. It's the beginning of a disciple's life, which is filled with God's grace to go and change the world, to bring it closer to the reality God created it to be.

WHEN SHOULD YOU BEGIN?

We start Confirmation preparation at the end of a teen's freshman year in high school. It normally concludes at the end of their sophomore year. That was decided before I was hired, and I didn't question it because that was my experience growing up.

Right now the timing of Confirmation is a hot topic in the Church in the United States. While I enjoy what we do in the high school years, I don't have a strong opinion about the best age for Confirmation. Of course there are both advantages and disadvantages to confirming at any age.

DURING HIGH SCHOOL

Advantages

High school students have the capacity to grasp the meaning of the sacrament. They have some independence and the ability to apply what they are learning in everyday life. It's also a natural season of maturing when they are preparing in fairly explicit ways for adulthood, so why can't the Church help them do the same?

Disadvantages

Most teenagers are beginning to solidify their beliefs and values. By the time many of them reach the second year of high school, they have decided already what they believe, particularly with regard to how much time and effort they want to put into religious practice. Challenging their beliefs and practice in these years might push them further away from the Church. Because most of them control much of their own schedule, they tend to be overstretched and overbooked. Consequently, it's hard to even get their attention.

DURING MIDDLE SCHOOL

Advantages

If you confirm in middle school, parents will be more engaged in the program. Many students in the middle school years are more open to adult perspectives and guidance than they might be in early high school when peer influence intensifies. They tend to have less control of their own schedules and are often less resistant to participation.

Disadvantages

It's easy to both overwhelm and underwhelm students of this age all at the same time. Because they are not yet focused on discovering just what their place is in the world or will become, they may not yet have a strong capacity for exploring the meaning of discipleship and of the sacrament of Confirmation. You will be able to plant good seeds of faith and relationship with Christ and his Church, but the need for very strong follow-up is crucial.

AT THE AGE OF REASON (WITH THE RESTORED ORDER OF INITIATION)

Advantages

Restoring the order of initiation for children mirrors what happens when adults join the Church through the Rite of Christian Initiation of Adults (RCIA). Restored order also underscores the Church's teaching that Eucharist completes initiation into the Church and is the sign of full union with the Church. Instead of spending years preparing students for Confirmation, you can focus on helping them live informed and sustained by its graces. Confirmation early in life (at or about the age of reason, which is generally accepted as seven years old) often helps free both parents and children from thinking of the sacrament as the end goal of religious formation program. Rather, it becomes a true beginning point, an initiation. In a very practical way, this timing eliminates the chaos that comes with a teenager's schedule and allows those leading the process to work with children who are often far more open to exploring religious practice and belief.

Disadvantages

While more families will likely be willing to go through preparation and receive the sacrament, a distinctive approach to sacramental preparation needs to evolve to prepare students this young for

Confirmation. Parishes will also need to address the question of how to keep these very young children and their families engaged in the life of the Church.

I don't know if there is a perfect age. And I think if that's where the focus is, all you will find is frustration. No matter what age children are confirmed where you are, the question you must probe is: What is supporting it?

The answer is healthy children's ministry and student ministry. When you have healthy programs for the children and youth of your parish that support and ground sacramental preparation, then you give them an on-and-off ramp. It's not *when* you start the process for sacramental prep; rather, it's what you do around it that matters. At Church of the Nativity we want to set a foundation that creates a thirst. Our hope is that through our small groups, ministry opportunities, and age-appropriate programs, our youth will want to know what's next and how they can get closer to Christ.

That might sound like a pipe dream, but it's a goal worth working to attain. It fuels the attitude *you get to do this* and eliminates the pressure of *you have to do this*.

While there are different ways to grow healthy children's and student ministries, I recommend reading *Rebuilt* and *Rebuilding Youth Ministry* for tools and tips.

Growing healthy children's and youth ministries doesn't mean you give up on sacramental preparation until you have the rest of your ministries in place. It does mean keeping in mind these layers of care and attention as you take kids and teenagers deeper in their faith. While constructing a powerful sacramental process, meet kids and teens early on in their faith lives and stick with them into adulthood. Keep working at building a foundation, and when it comes time to go deeper you'll find that you have kids and teenagers who are more excited and engaged.

INFORMATIONAL MEETING

To help people move from *have to* to *get to*, you need to make sure they are coming in to Confirmation with a clear expectation. Your first opportunity to change the paradigm is at the informational meeting for teens and parents as you prepare to get the program year underway. This meeting should be a combination of inspiration and application. This is important because it sets the tone and lays out the path. It's your opportunity to set expectations.

At our parish, this meeting isn't mandatory, but we strongly encourage people to come. We advertise it as an opportunity to hear the entire plan and ask any questions they have about preparing for Confirmation. Our hope is that parents and teens walk away discussing this next step in the teens' faith lives.

Your informational meeting should be unlike any regular meeting. In fact it should be the meeting of meetings. That means attending to basics, such as having an agenda, starting on time, recruiting people to help you, and ending on time.

I know talking about an informational meeting seems unnecessary, but the truth is that this meeting sets the tone for the rest of your preparation. Part of the reason Confirmation preparation seems like a laborious task is because it's filled with people who don't want to be there run by people who want to get through it as quickly as possible.

After you plan for the basics, it's important to fill your agenda with content that's going to dispel any myths and compel both teens and their parents to engage in the journey ahead. That means addressing the purpose of this sacramental gift. And that's important to address because when you ask most teenagers what Confirmation is, they'll give you answers such as these:

- It means I get to be an adult in the parish.
- It makes me a better person.
- I want to get my parents off of my back.

- I need to do it to get married in the Church.
- It's the last part of my religious education.

The problem with these answers is that they result from many Catholics not understanding what the sacrament offers us. In the end people will make their own assumptions on why Confirmation preparation exists, but the *Catechism of the Catholic Church* tells us something quite explicit. It tells us that the sacraments of Christian initiation—Baptism, Confirmation, and the Eucharist—lay the foundations of every Christian life.

> The sharing in the divine nature given to men through the grace of Christ bears a certain likeness to the origin, development, and nourishing of natural life. The faithful are born anew by Baptism, strengthened by the sacrament of Confirmation, and receive in the Eucharist the food of eternal life. By means of these sacraments of Christian initiation, they thus receive in increasing measure the treasures of the divine life and advance toward the perfection of charity.
> —*Catechism of the Catholic Church,* 1212

In other words, preparing for Confirmation is preparing the next generation for a change in the way they approach life. Before Jesus commissioned his followers to go forth to make disciples, he said to them, "But you will receive power when the holy Spirit comes upon you, and you will be my witnesses in Jerusalem, throughout Judea and Samaria, and to the ends of the earth" (Acts 1:8). They were going to go from followers to advocates of Jesus Christ. And they were going to do that with the power of the Holy Spirit. If you can help your Confirmation candidates to know they are being offered the same promise and commission, it's safe to say they would approach preparation with a much different perspective.

That's a lot to grasp, and I admit that I still have to wrestle with it from time to time. You are asking teenagers to go into the world and share something that can be polarizing and even controversial. And when teens hear that's how serious we are, it can be a lot to digest. It's important not to discourage them but to clarify the path ahead. If teenagers and their parents understand what's expected of them and what they can expect, their attitude will change. You have the ability to change what once was a broken process into a season of life that they will come to treasure.

If people are aware of what really happens before they partake in this journey, they'll stop seeing it as just an annoying checklist item. Confirmation will lose its graduation stigma only if we begin to preach what it is and what it can be. There will be times when you'll feel as if you are preaching to dry bones and speaking into the wind. But the message of *you get to do this* is one that needs to be repeated. Because when they *get to do this*, they'll see the privilege and joy that comes with living a life overflowing with God's awesome grace.

Part II
BUILDING A STRATEGY

3
GET THE RIGHT CANDIDATES

The centurion said in reply, "Lord, I am not worthy to have you enter under my roof; only say the word and my servant will be healed. . . ." When Jesus heard this, he was amazed and said to those following him, "Amen, I say to you, in no one in Israel have I found such faith."
—Matthew 8:8, 10

It's hard to get people to embark on a journey when they are reluctant to travel. When it comes to Confirmation preparation many of us encounter teenagers who just aren't ready. Instead of challenging them to step up or step back, we often choose to put them through the motions anyway. In the end we compromise the integrity of the program, diminish the celebration of the sacrament, and create more work for ourselves.

When I was initially asked to take on Church of the Nativity's high school ministry on top of the middle school program I was already doing, I didn't worry. I remember thinking that it wouldn't be a problem because middle school youth ministry is far more chaotic than the high school work would be.

I was right. Middle school youth ministry is more chaotic. But I would take that chaos any day over the tension I felt my first night of high school ministry. Everyone in Confirmation preparation had to attend our high school program to meet an attendance requirement. Every week teens had to sign in so we could prove they had been in attendance at least 80 percent of the time. This meant the majority of high school students present were there because they *had to be there.*

The teenagers who wanted to be there were few and far between. And, sadly, they didn't stick around very long. The reason they didn't stick around was that they felt the tension too. Those students who had to be there didn't want to be there, and they weren't afraid to hide those feelings.

Each time we met I encountered three distinct student reactions to having to be there: (1) stares that screamed, *Why are you doing this to me?* (2) heads on tables, and (3) active opposition. In this latter group, teens yawned, sighed, coughed, or made any audible sound trying desperately to let me know, *This is booooooring!*

Now, don't get me wrong—there were teens in our Confirmation program that wanted to receive the sacrament. They were just afraid to show that publicly because any sign of enthusiasm or encouragement was a major violation of the unwritten social code.

I tried everything I could to create energy. I pulled out every activity that had worked with the middle school students. I attempted talking one-on-one with teens I deemed leaders in an effort to win them over, hoping they would help me out. Yet no matter how hard I worked toward improving the program, I was met with resistance. Two things were quickly apparent: the system was broken, and unwilling participants were in the room.

I know I've said that Confirmation has a systems problem and not a people problem. But one of the key hurdles to overcome on the way to effective programing is the fact that teenagers walk in not ready for what we are about to ask of them. And although they aren't ready, we so often push them through. By pushing them through we create a negative experience for all involved.

While we ought not refuse a sacrament except for grave reasons, we can and ought to help prepare people for the reception of the sacraments in a manner that attends to the realities of where each is on his or her journey of faith. We must ensure they are ready both because they understand the meaning of the sacrament and because their hearts are open to deeper relationship with Christ. So how can we help teens discern when they are ready to open their hearts and minds and begin preparing for Confirmation?

At our parish teens don't enroll for Confirmation preparation; instead, they apply for it. We believe an application process is necessary because it brings formality. That formality causes people to slow down and think, *Am I doing what I want to be doing?* Our process is not difficult, but I suspect it is more extensive than what one finds in most parishes. The structure of our application is outlined here, and a sample of it can be found in appendix A of this book.

CONFIRMATION APPLICATION

I: PERSONAL INFORMATION

In the first section we gather basic information such as the applicant's name, address, phone number, and e-mail address. We ask how they prefer we keep in touch with both candidates and their parents. Since people communicate in a variety of ways we want to know if the best way to make contact is a phone call, a text, or an e-mail. There is no way we want people falling through the cracks because we e-mailed and they really don't check their mail very often.

II: TEEN AND PARENT ESSAYS

In the second section we go deeper by asking candidates and their parents to each write a five-hundred-word essay answering one of two questions.

Teens choose from the following two options:

What Type of Christian Man or Woman Do You Envision Being in the Future?

The purpose of this question is for us to get an idea of what it means to these young people to be a disciple of Jesus Christ. If we are in the business of growing disciples, we need to know how they approach the idea of being one or, indeed, *if* they have thought much about it.

What Steps Do You Need to Take to Get Closer to God?

We ask teens this question to get an idea of what their relationship with God looks like. For some of them this is the first time anyone has ever asked them this question. This answer will help us know what goals they might want to set. It will tell us what they think is most important in having a personal relationship with Christ.

Parents choose from the following two options:

How Have You Shared with Your Teen the Importance of This Sacrament?

We don't assume that parents and teens are on the same page when it comes to preparing for Confirmation. Even if they have a deep and profound conversation, we know that an adult is going to approach this differently. Our goal with this question is to get an idea of what's been said. We want to know the ideas that are shaping a teen's perspective of the journey they are going to take.

What Is the Hope or Vision You Have for Your Child after He or She Receives This Sacrament?

This question is all about learning what parents want for their teen. Answers vary from, "I want my teen to learn more about the Church" to, "This is my last chance to teach my teen about God." I personally love this question because this is where we learn the fears, hopes, and dreams that parents have for their teens.

We have teens and parents write an essay because we want to know exactly where they are on the journey. We want to know whom we are working with and something of the raw material of their faith lives. The point of these essays is not to test their knowledge but to gain insight to what's going on in their lives.

After doing this for years you begin to recognize when parents and teens are writing what they think you want to hear and when they are writing what they want you to hear. At first, we got a little pushback about this essay writing, but once we learned to sit down and explain our intentions, we found that parents and teens get excited. They are more invested because they realize that someone truly wants to hear them. When we know where people are starting, it's easier for us to meet them and help them take the right next step.

III: SPONSOR AND NAME

Sponsors

My sponsor was my uncle Bobby. I've been blessed to have uncles and aunts who have openly shared their faith with me. One of the reasons I chose my uncle was that he was willing to share the way God was interacting in his life. At the time I knew I wanted to be able to talk about God and the Church with the same kind of enthusiasm.

During preparation we don't ask much of the sponsor in our program at Nativity. We just ask a sponsor to check in with the candidate and keep them in their prayers. We do this to challenge the candidate's decision. It's not that we don't believe they've made the best choice, but we want them to truly understand the role of a sponsor.

The way we help them do that is by modeling the role through their mentor, the person who will walk with them through preparation. I write more about mentors later in this book, but for now understand that these individuals are chosen and trained by the parish staff to accompany, coach, and guide our Confirmation candidates through the preparation process. Sponsors are individuals who have a special place in the teens' lives by standing with them at Confirmation and continuing to accompany them and guide them in the years that follow. Many times we've seen a candidate keep the same person he or she lists as a sponsor on the application. But we've also seen many of them make a change because they've found someone who will invest in them the way their mentor did.

We ask for the name and sponsor early on to create a conversation that will lead to a deeper understanding. If a candidate is not sure what to put down, we tell them it's okay but to be prepared to talk about it.

Confirmation Names

I had no clue what I wanted my Confirmation name to be. I remember the deadline to pick was coming up and my mom pleaded with me to just pick one. I decided to do what any mature Catholic would do—I played Bible roulette. I decided, in my awesome teenage wisdom, that opening to a random page of the Bible would reveal to me the name God wanted me to pick. The first time around, I opened up to Jesus. My mom convinced me that this would not be appropriate and that my strategy wasn't wise. I agreed with her regarding the name; however, I decided to give it one more try. I opened the Bible to Ezekiel, and immediately I knew that was it.

I didn't know why it was the name for me; I had never read the book of Ezekiel. I don't even think I knew at the time that he was a prophet in the Old Testament. But something in my heart told me this was the right name for me.

How I chose Ezekiel wasn't wise, but I'm glad that's the name I chose. As I've gotten to know the story of Ezekiel, I realize God was communicating early on to me that one day talking in front of teenagers would sometimes feel a lot like Ezekiel must have felt talking to that field of dry bones!

Teenagers choose Confirmation names for a variety of reasons. We ask them about a name on the application so we can create a dialogue. We want to ask them, "Why is that name important to you?" Whether they keep it or change it is irrelevant as long as they know why. Of course, they don't have to choose a name at all. The Rite of Confirmation doesn't call for this, but it is a tradition that teens seem to like and provides a great opportunity to talk with them about role models and how they see their relationship with God.

IV: COMMITMENT FORM

The way we protect the integrity of the sacrament is by having both teens and parents sign a commitment form. On that form we list the expectations we have for parents and teenagers. We want them to pause, think about the journey ahead, and honestly answer the question, Am I ready to take the next step?

We understand that life happens and that once you enter into the process teens will be challenged by schedules, stress, and doubts. We've had teenagers lose loved ones; we've had parents go through divorce and families overcome incredible adversity. We know that the commitment will be tested and tried. In the end we only ask that they commit to trying their best and trusting us to walk with them.

We're always trying to improve our application. To see what we've used, see appendix A. It's no longer a paper document that we e-mail or hand out; it's something done online. We're constantly asking ourselves, Are we getting the best information possible? The truth is, while we like our application process, we know it isn't perfect.

In the end if you want the right people as a part of your program you can't just rely on an application. An application is a tool to meet people where they are. The way we get the right people is by creating a culture where people know they don't have to do this. Those are scary words, especially to parents when we tell their teens at the information meeting. Most parents want their teens to go through preparation, so when the youth minister is saying, "No, you really don't have to," they panic. You can see their concern until I reframe the situation and invite them to realize how fortunate they are that they get to do this.

I don't know why it's attractive to hear that phrase. Maybe it's because we've removed a burden. Maybe we've helped teenagers realize they are in control of this journey and that God loves them enough to give them free will. All I do know is that by repeating that phrase over and over again, we've seen a difference. Where do we see the difference? We see it in the essays they write.

Early on, parents and teens gave us those textbook kind of answers such as "I want to be seen as an adult or mature in my faith." Those are great answers, but they aren't personal. The more we tell teens and parents "you get to do this," the more we hear responses such as "I want to really get to know what God has in store for my life/my child's life." And when you see those answers, you can't help but get excited about the process.

When you get people who are motivated and engaged, it brings enthusiasm to your volunteers, your program, and even the Church. When you start the process on a strong footing, you have momentum, and that changes and challenges the parish to be a movement of disciples.

As you think about your Confirmation program I want to challenge you to answer this question: How do we get the right people on board? Look at your enrollment process. Think about the questions you need to ask, the information you need to gather, and how you can remind people that a relationship with God is a choice that leads to the best life ever.

4
ELIMINATE CLASSROOMS

And what you heard from me through many witnesses entrust to faithful people who will have the ability to teach others as well. Bear your share of hardship along with me like a good soldier of Christ Jesus.

—2 Timothy 2:2–3

The more insight, truth, and wisdom young people can receive, the stronger their faith will become. Unfortunately, we've too often placed our hopes in a piece of curriculum that comes in a comprehensive booklet or in a well-produced video program that someone has promised will satisfy all their faith-formation needs. To share deep, profound, and life-changing truth, you need men and women who love God and are passionate about caring for the next generation. You need faithful adults willing and able to accompany your young people on the road to mature discipleship.

I can't recall what Confirmation curriculum we used in the parish where I grew up. What I do remember is my teacher, Mrs. Smith. She's a saint in my opinion because she put up with a lot of my adolescent and immature behavior. Each week she showed up, excited to share with my fellow candidates and me her relationship with God. She faithfully accompanied us as teacher, guide, and companion in the faith.

If you think about how your faith has been shaped, I suspect you can recall most clearly influential people or groups of people who showed you what it's like to live as a follower of Jesus Christ. Someone inspired, challenged, or influenced you to go deeper into your faith. For me there was Mrs. Smith, who showed enthusiasm for her faith and the local church. Even if I didn't deserve it she showed me respect and displayed God's love. While I was happy to be done with the classes, I was going to miss how she invested in me.

When creating a Confirmation program you want to make sure you have people who are committed to being invested and understand that teens are not perfect. Teenagers are going to be more receptive to adults who are showing enthusiasm. That does not mean they need to be goofy and energetic; it does mean loving *what* they are teaching and *whom* they are teaching.

But Confirmation needs more than teachers. Confirmation needs men and women who are going to take the time to listen and walk with a student through difficult questions and enlightening moments. For me one such person was Father Al Bischoff (better known as Father B), a Jesuit priest on Xavier University's campus. I knew him after I was confirmed, when I was in college.

I'll never forget coming back from a party at the crack of dawn and seeing him sitting on a bench outside the dorm with a smile on his face. At first I wondered if he was going to give me a hard time for being out late, but instead he greeted me with a "Good to see you saint." It immediately disarmed me, and instead of feeling shame I felt love. I cracked a smile, said a soft hello, and went back to my dorm room.

I remember sharing the encounter with a friend, and he informed me that this was not unusual behavior from Father B. Every day he greets students with "Good to see you saint." It didn't make sense; why would he greet us with such a positive salutation perfectly knowing we had been anything but saintly?

Eventually I had the opportunity to ask him, "What's with the 'saint' comment?" His response was priceless. He said, "Well, we all have the potential to be saints, and I want people to know that. And I'm not great when it comes to remembering names."

Father B saw the good in me even when I could not. I wanted to learn what he was seeing, and so I decided to get to know him. It started out with asking simple questions about Xavier basketball and academics. Over time the questions would go deeper and so would the conversation. By the time I graduated I saw him as a mentor, someone I could go to whenever I couldn't figure it out on my own. He was a wonderful companion for me as my faith matured during those years.

Confirmation is an opportunity for us to show the next generation that they have the potential to be saints. When you sit in a classroom and crack open a textbook, the focus is on the content and not the individual. While the information you need to teach is important, if the individual isn't receptive to that information then it's useless. A healthy Confirmation program has adult volunteers whom teenagers trust and respect. When the relationship is strong, then a teenager will be receptive to what the adult has to say.

To facilitate these strong relationships and eliminate the classroom, you need to look at the delivery system of the content you want your candidates to embrace. At Nativity, we build our delivery around small groups and mentoring relationships.

SMALL GROUPS AND MENTORING

You might be wondering, *If you eliminate the classroom, then where and how do candidates meet?* There are several ways you can make your programs more relational. When I assumed responsibility for Confirmation prep at Church of the Nativity, the model was faith formation in small groups. The groups were comprised of six to eight students and were led by two adults, trained for this ministry. They were single-sex groups and met on a weekly basis.

The environment was casual: there were no textbooks, teenagers sat on couches, and information was shared in the form of a conversation. Our goal was to communicate that this was different from a school setting. We wanted teens to connect this experience to the kind of experience they might have hanging out at a friend's house.

This model meant that leaders were equipped with content that didn't seem intimidating or overwhelming. There were no textbooks or workbooks. We gave them materials to prepare ahead of time, and the most they brought with them was a sheet of paper with some questions and talking points. We didn't want leaders to lecture the candidates; we wanted them to facilitate a conversation.

The program had bright spots. Teenagers were connecting with the leaders, and they were building relationships. A deep sense of community formed in the small groups unless there were one or two students who didn't want to be there. When we identified these reluctant teens we tried to work with them outside of the group.

Small groups are an excellent place to start when it comes to remodeling your Confirmation program. Unfortunately, there will be teens that are going through the process reluctantly. If you cannot change their minds and hearts quickly, it can hurt the rest of the group.

When we were able to focus on the reluctant students we saw progress. We were able to address their feelings and help them discern whether or not they were ready to receive the sacrament. As we got better at addressing the needs of these students one-on-one, we started to realize the value of mentoring relationships and so began the transition from small groups to mentoring as the core of our system. Not only did mentoring help us focus on the challenging students, but it allowed us to provide needed attention to the quieter ones as well. Teens could not hide behind their more talkative counterparts as they could so easily in small groups.

Our mentoring program is simple. We pair teenagers with an adult who is living as a disciple of Christ, passionate about sharing the Catholic faith, and interested in investing in the next generation. Our mentors model for students what to look for in a sponsor. They become trusted companions and vibrant examples of genuine discipleship.

Our intention is not to make the mentor a sponsor (although they could become one in the end) but to show the candidate what that relationship could and should look like. It can be a difficult picture to paint because being a sponsor is such an honored role. People are usually chosen out of respect to honor family or friends, and it's become a title with little or no responsibility. To be fair there is no sponsor school or training. Usually we hope we can prepare someone to be a sponsor at the same time that we are preparing the teenager for the sacrament.

Ideally when a teenager picks a sponsor that person should know what to do. Instead of preparing a sponsor to take on a teenager, shouldn't we show the next generation what to look for in a sponsor? If you can do that, then you give them a tool that no curriculum can provide. You give them someone who will hold them accountable to go and grow deeper in their faith and gain a wider view of the Christian life.

WHAT DOES MENTORING LOOK LIKE?

Mentors meet with teenagers one-on-one at least seven times over the span of eight months. We've tried having the process go beyond eight months but have found that the candidates (and even some of the mentors) have burned out from the duration. If a candidate and mentor decide they want to meet more, we certainly encourage them to do so.

Again, mentoring allows us to focus on the candidate. When you are meeting one-on-one the meetings are slightly more intense and you are able to cover more material. Candidates can't hide behind other classmates, and they have the ability to open up without fear of being judged by their peers.

The idea of one-on-one can be intimidating. Some people ask about safety and what the diocese might require to ensure our students are safe. All of our mentors go through the necessary background checks and training. First, a mentor needs to be referred. Who refers them makes a big difference. If it's a coworker or someone I know, the referral holds more weight. Next, each of our mentors is interviewed. It's during this time that we ask their intentions for getting involved. We do not want adults who are trying to be friends with teenagers. We do not want adults who feel teenagers need another disciplinarian. We want adults who see themselves as a guide for the next generation. They know why their Catholic faith is important, and they know it takes work but that in the end it's worth it.

We are also looking for adults who are going to connect not only with teenagers but with their parents as well. These mentors are partners for parents. It is important that parents feel comfortable approaching mentors and that mentors feel comfortable including parents throughout the process.

Before any candidate meets with his or her mentor one-on-one, we bring everyone together for our kickoff gathering we call Meet Your Mentor. At this meeting we break the ice, get everyone on the same page, and build trust. If after this encounter a parent, teenager, or mentor has a concern about the relationship, we make the necessary adjustments. By the end of the meeting everyone is clear on what comes next, and they've scheduled as many of their one-on-one meetings as possible.

When the candidates and mentors start meeting, we really begin to see the teenagers open up and grow. During this time, mentors work through content, but again it's how they share it that starts the journey. They share content as guides and companions on the journey of faith.

While a candidate might elect to meet with a mentor at church, we also encourage them to meet in public places such as coffee shops or fast-food restaurants. Our hope is that this creates comfort with discussing faith outside the walls of a church building. And sometimes it's about meeting in not just a public place but a place and style that is significant to the mentor.

One of our mentors is a chef, and she asked her candidates to pick a couple of dishes they would like to learn how to make. Each time they meet she uses the kitchen as her classroom to share not only incredible cooking tips but life skills as well.

Another one of our mentors is passionate about serving in Baltimore and introduced his Confirmation candidates to a service opportunity where they could meet men recovering from addiction.

Every year he plans at least two trips to serve with his candidates and then discusses life and faith afterward.

We have mentors who share their love of the outdoors by taking their candidates on hikes. And there are mentors who will give their candidates devotionals and studies that help them in their own faith journey.

Ours is an unconventional but extremely effective model, but our mentors seriously impact the next generation of Catholic disciples. We love that our mentors find creative and new ways to connect with the teenagers and parents. We want to change the perception that faith formation is relegated to a classroom. We want to show people that how we make disciples really doesn't have any limits.

BUILD YOUR TEAM

Whether you choose a small-group or mentoring model, you need to find the right people to invest in the candidates. You might think that finding these people will be like looking for leprechauns, but they are probably closer than you think, and there are doubtless more of them in your parish than you expect. Unless your church is completely empty on the weekend, there are men and women in your church community that love God, love others, and love their faith. They might not seem the most likely people for the task at first glance, but they do exist. Seeking men and women to serve as mentors might seem daunting, but don't be overwhelmed by recruiting.

Pray for Them

Your Confirmation mentors are important people. Pray for them. Ask God to ready their hearts when you ask them. Ask God to help you recognize opportunities to meet them. Praying for your mentors might sound cliché, but you want to make sure you can find people you trust. You are introducing them into an intense relationship with teenagers, and you want to make sure you are all on the same page.

Be Present

The best way to find practicing Catholics is by being present when Catholics are practicing their faith. That means standing outside the front door of your church on a Sunday greeting people as they come in. Shake hands, greet them audibly, and make some kind of connection. Over time strike up a conversation with one of them and get to know her or him personally.

Not only will you start to identify potential mentors, but also they'll be able to identify you. They won't be wondering who this youth minister or DRE is who's inviting them to be a part of the program.

Seek Referrals

Why do we try things out for the first time? We are willing to try because we've had referrals. You will go to a certain movie, restaurant, or yoga class because someone told you, "It was great—you need to check it out!"

If going up to a random person seems too intimidating, ask coworkers, your pastor, parents, and even the teens themselves for the names of people they think would make great mentors. Let them know what you're looking for so they aren't just throwing out any name. And then when you call that person say, "So-and-so recommended that I call you to share with you a little about our Confirmation program." When people know that another person referred them, it builds confidence and helps them hear the invitation in a more personal way that often has greater impact than an invitation unconnected to someone they already know.

Building your team will take time. Don't rush the process; just find the right people. In chapter 9 we'll talk more about what to look for in your leaders. You might feel overwhelmed, and the idea of finding enough people could seem impossible.

Starting with a mentoring program might seem overwhelming. You might wonder, *How do I find enough people for all the candidates I currently have in the program?* If you cannot find enough mentors then look at a small-group model. Small groups gave us the ability to find the right people, create a culture, and slowly but surely recruit enough people to shift to our current one-on-one model. For more on small groups I recommend reading my book *Rebuilding Youth Ministry: Ten Practical Strategies for Catholic Parishes.*

MENTOR TRAINING

Mentoring the next generation sounds simple and intimidating at the same time. To help our mentors have the confidence to sit down and share what's helped them grow, we spend time training before they begin meeting with their candidates. During that time we focus on the following three areas.

Community

We have several mentors serving in our Confirmation program. Because they do not serve together at the same time and in the same location, it can sometimes feel to them that they are on their own. Forming community among the mentors can be a challenge, and that's why we make sure mentors connect with each other through trainings and check-in meetings. They need to know who else is serving so they can lean on one another. We make sure they spend time getting to know one another so they can call each other for collaboration and support. To help with this, we recruit coaches to connect mentors with one another. This effectively extends my capacity to address the needs of our mentors.

Communication

Because there are so many people involved in the Confirmation process, we stress with our mentors the importance of communication. If your ministers or volunteers aren't communicating with one another, the team you are trying to form will fall apart. We want them connecting not only with their candidates but with the parents, sponsors, and each other as well. The more everyone communicates, the less likely it is that anyone will be confused. The most successful situation is when mentors work with the entire family to help their children go deeper in a relationship with Jesus Christ.

Vision

There are going to be times when it's difficult for the mentor to schedule a meeting with the candidate. There will be seasons when mentors are personally challenged in their spiritual life. We want our mentors to know why this ministry is so important. We want them to remember that they are planting seeds that might not produce fruit for years. We want them to know that although the work can be hard, the outcome is worth it. To remind them of this we share stories such as this one with them:

> Dear Bishop Madden,
>
> I plan to be completely honest in this letter. I see no reason to lie or make things up. It will get quite personal, too. Over the past year, my faith has had many ups and downs. Sometimes it seems like there were more downs. It has been a very interesting journey to say the least.
>
> Starting out the Confirmation process, I really didn't have much faith at all. I knew there was some kind of higher power that was up there, but I didn't know or care what it was. The only reason I was getting confirmed was to make my parents happy. I didn't really want anything to do with the Church or God or religion in general. This feeling only intensified during the trip to Steubenville.
>
> On that trip I was rooming with a girl I won't bother naming. My three roommates and I had a very deep and personal conversation about religion and such one night. If I'm honest, at that point I considered myself to be an atheist. I didn't believe in God, I didn't want anything to do with God, and most of all, I didn't want to be on that trip hearing about God every single day. I shared this with my roommates, and

two of the three simply shared that they hoped I found my faith again. The third, however, didn't approve of my lack of faith. She basically told me that my life would just get worse and God would punish me for not having faith in him. She didn't even give me a chance to explain myself. After sharing this, she stared at me like I was diseased, and continued the conversation without me.

Now let me explain why I had those feelings towards religion. I had recently been through a lot (and I mean a lot) of hardships, and I thought, "Well if God really cared about me, this wouldn't be happening to me." I'll give a short synopsis of what had happened. My mother has MS, and it had been getting worse at that time. My aunt's back was getting increasingly worse. My grandmother was in the hospital. A close friend of mine had attempted suicide. And my depression and anxiety were through the roof. I basically had given up any hope of things getting better, and my faith diminished. Why would God put my family and me through this pain?

Skipping ahead to August, just as my roommate said, life just got worse. All I could think about was how bad life was and how much I hated the Church. I eventually attempted suicide, landing myself in Sheppard Pratt [a psychiatric hospital] for most of the month. After surviving an extreme overdose, I realized maybe there is a God watching over me. I became less angry with the Church, and much less angry with myself. I began going to Mass again, and I began praying again. I was starting to slowly get my faith back. I still did not want to get confirmed, however. Until I met my mentor Lisa.

Lisa is probably one of the most understanding and supportive women I have ever met. When I explained my reservations towards God and religion, she understood completely. She has helped me incredibly in my journey toward Confirmation, and I'm actually extremely excited for Confirmation Mass. Lisa helped me figure out what I wanted out of this process, and she helped me realize that God puts us through hardships to test our strength and our faith. I have a newfound trust in God, and I'm excited to see what He has in store for me.

This has been my interesting, crazy journey through the Confirmation process. As I mentioned before, I am honestly very excited to get confirmed, and I can't wait to better my relationship with God.

This letter reminds us not only that is life change happening for our teenagers but also that God is using our mentors to do amazing things. When they see the vision and the level of commitment to serve, the next generation becomes solid.

5
MOVE FROM TEXTBOOKS TO TOOLS

"Come to me, all you who labor and are burdened, and I will give you rest. Take my yoke upon you and learn from me, for I am meek and humble of heart; and you will find rest for yourselves. For my yoke is easy, and my burden light."

—Matthew 11:28–30

Once you have your team in place you need to start looking at equipping them for the journey ahead. To do that it's not just about what they know but also about how it's shared with the next generation.

I'll never forget my first car. It was a white Toyota Camry, and I named her Cynthia. I loved Cynthia because she symbolized freedom. I no longer had to rely on friends to get me from point A to point B. I didn't have to share with my sisters or my mom. I had my own car, and I could do whatever I wanted with it, including taking care of repairs.

The first time I had a flat tire I figured changing it was something I could do on my own. No one had ever shown me how to change it, but I pulled out the manual from the glove box and thought, *This should be simple, right?* And it was:

Step 1: Get the car jack, tire iron, and spare out of the trunk.
Step 2: Loosen lug nuts on flat tire with tire iron.

Step 2: Loosen lug nuts on flat tire?
Step 2: Loosen lug nuts on flat tire!

For some reason I couldn't get past step 2, and I was completely confused. I checked the manual again; I had followed the instructions word for word, so what the heck was going on?

There I sat on the side of the road, confused, and just scratching my head when someone pulled up and asked if I needed help. I said, "Yeah."

He had a go at step 2 with the same result; that's when he said, "I think you need some WD40." I said, "What?" He said, "Your lug nuts probably have a little rust on them. You need some oil to loosen that; let me get you some."

He went to his trunk, pulled out some of the stuff, and sprayed the lug nuts. A few minutes later I could easily move past step 2 and continue to change my tire successfully.

Life is easy in a vacuum, but reality is much tougher. Too often we present catechesis as something that should be simple. The truth is life is messy. It's complicated, and while what we share with our candidates is truth, life is going to make applying it and embracing it quite challenging. It's not just about teaching information; it's also about showing application.

The obstacles to faith that teens face will come in many forms. They'll be challenged by things like:

- the friend or a classmate who has a different set of beliefs
- a tragedy that shakes their foundation (i.e., death or divorce)
- a busy schedule that distracts them from focusing on God
- temptations that convince them to put their own desires first
- seemingly constant pressure to focus on worldly success and security

We need to prepare the candidates with the right tools to face these challenging realities of life in twenty-first-century America. The document *Seal of the Spirit* distributed by the Archdiocese of Baltimore reads in part:

> The immediate preparation process for Confirmation must be understood within the context of life long catechesis and within the context of ongoing adolescent catechesis. It is not an appropriate time to bear the weight of providing all information and formation in faith necessary for adult living. It should thoroughly inform and prepare the candidate for participation in the Rite of Confirmation, its components, symbols, and effects. It should focus on completion of initiation and on active membership in the church community, as well as invite young people to a lived discipleship in the world. Like all catechesis, it should focus on the person of Jesus, draw its lessons from the scripture, and invite them to closer relationship and modeling of him in everyday life.
>
> —*Seal of the Spirit*, 14

Confirmation prep shouldn't be a class that candidates need to pass; it should be an apprenticeship in how to live life in and outside of the Church. The first step we took to go from information to application was eliminating the textbook and looking at tools.

One of the first places we looked was Doug Field's resource, *H.A.B.I.T.S.: Discipleship Tools to Help Students Cultivate Spiritual Growth . . . On Their Own*. H.A.B.I.T.S. is an acronym for

Hang time with God
Accountability with another believer
Bible memorization
Involvement with the church body
Tithing commitment
Study scripture

This resource came on a CD filled with instructions, exercises, and tools for each habit. Some of the exercises were devotionals. A few of the tools included Bible memory verses students could hang on a key tag. Its purpose was to give teenagers timeless practices and tools to help them in their faith journey.

This resource was incredible because it gave our Confirmation candidates tools and clear steps on how to apply faith in their everyday life. We also recognized that we could better align it with our Catholic faith. So to stay with the acronym, we changed Bible memorization into Bible studies and changed the *S* at the end to stand for *sacraments.*

This resource gave us the ability to create talking points between the mentors and candidates. Mentors could say, "Hey, this is how I pray; check out this tool that I use." Over time mentors would suggest other tools such as lectio divina, various devotionals, and other exercises that gave our catalog of resources depth.

Some might argue that we should have taught the students more history and information about their faith, but we felt these were the six essential habits that would encourage them to go further on their own. It was easy to remember and simple to share, and we started to see teenagers pick up the habits. They were asking their mentors for Bibles, we saw them engaging in the sacraments, and they were getting involved in ministry.

Today our content has evolved from H.A.B.I.T.S. into something we call S.T.E.P.S., which stands for

> **S**erve in ministry and missions
> **T**ithe through sacrificial giving
> **E**ngage in small-group relationships
> **P**ractice prayer and the sacraments
> **S**hare through invest and invite

Why did we make the change? Our church staff realized that what we were teaching in kids' ministry, adult ministry, and student ministry was similar but slightly different. And that is okay to a certain point. But we felt that if we really wanted to be growing disciples who were growing other disciples, we needed to be one church with one message. Toward that goal, we asked ourselves, What are the behaviors of a disciple of Jesus Christ? What tools and opportunities will nurture those behaviors? What needs to change so that everything we do promotes these behaviors?

We then formulated S.T.E.P.S. and began to apply this tool across all our ministries. In chapters 7 through 11, I'll break down S.T.E.P.S. further and explain the tools that we give our mentors. But we knew that by coming up with a discipleship path that was used throughout the church, we could help build a foundation that would help our Confirmation program to go deeper than before.

Not only were we giving our mentors tools instead of a textbook, but we were also providing them with resources that could be found throughout the entire fabric of our parish. Going from textbook to tools might seem complicated; however, it's quite simple. It starts by answering those questions we just covered:

What Are the Behaviors of a Disciple of Jesus Christ?

The list is limitless, and that can be a little overwhelming. My suggestion is that you meet with your parish's leadership and have a deep conversation on this subject.

If you can engage the leadership you will have an impact on every generation in your parish. When you can decide on the same disciplines, then you can start making an impact earlier. The earlier you begin, the deeper you can go with teenagers entering into preparation.

But if you have to start with teenagers, identify five to seven behaviors that can lead the candidates to develop other ones down the line. In other words, decide what disciplines promote self-growth and further exploration. A clear example is serving. A disciple of Jesus Christ serves because it's a behavior that follows through on what Jesus commanded when he told his followers, "I give you a new commandment: love one another. As I have loved you, so you also should love one another. This is how all will know that you are my disciples, if you have love for one another" (Jn 13:34–35).

Not only does service honor what Jesus taught us, but it's also something that is limitless. You can serve in a variety of ways in and outside the church. When you contribute your time to love others you will in return receive God's love. Use ours if you are not sure which habits or tools to embrace. After all we didn't invent them; they came right from the Bible.

What Tools and
Opportunities Will Nurture Those Behaviors?

Recall what happened in my tire-changing story because I didn't have the right information or the right tool. I didn't know about the rust, nor did I have the WD40. Imagine if, when I had the flat, I didn't have any of the right tools. In fact, imagine opening up your trunk to realize that there was no tire iron or spare. You would be lost.

Too often we tell Confirmation candidates to read scripture, pray daily, and serve others without giving them the proper tools for success. What we need to do is break it down and make these practices accessible. The purpose of developing tools and opportunities is to take something that can seem daunting (e.g., reading the Bible) and create an opportunity for success.

What you need to do with your team is find age-appropriate resources and opportunities that can help them slowly develop that Christlike habit. Again, my recommendation is try to introduce these tools earlier with younger kids so that you can go deeper with the older ones.

Where do you find these tools? You can find them in the Rebuilt Parish Association (rebuiltparishassociation.com) or find them in appendix B of this book. While you might find a few suggestions there, I encourage you to also talk with people in your parish who are already modeling Christ. Ask them what they do and use. Add it to your library, and build your toolbox.

What Needs to Change
So That Everything We Do Promotes These Behaviors?

This last question you need to answer is simple but requires facing some brutal truths. I recommend reading chapter 9, "Asking the Right Questions," in my book *Rebuilding Youth Ministry*. In that chapter I talk about how to evaluate a program and whether it's meeting your vision and mission.

There are probably a lot of great and memorable things your parish does for the next generation. However, if you do not promote behaviors that reflect a disciple of Jesus Christ then it will only work against your best efforts. So before you start adding items to your list, make sure you have gotten rid of the ones that will slow you down. If you can direct youth to opportunities that help them grow as disciples, then you will see the fruit of your labor.

Going from textbooks to tools means looking at more than what you are teaching; you need to also examine why and how you are teaching. Stepping away from a leader's guide or teacher manual may seem like a big move, but once you do you'll find there are endless ways of showing the next generation what it means to become growing disciples who are growing other disciples.

6

GIVE THEM
A BIGGER PICTURE

I praise you, because I am wonderfully made;
wonderful are your works!
My very self you know.

—Psalm 139:14

No matter where candidates are at the beginning of Confirmation preparation, it's definitely not the place for them to stay. God has given each and every one of us a vision that is bigger than what the world can offer to us. Confirmation preparation is an opportunity to introduce the next generation to that vision.

In high school I wanted to be a famous pianist like Billy Joel or Ben Folds. I spent hours practicing scales and theory. I dreamt about the sold-out concerts, world tours, and even my Grammy speech. Every day I sat down in front of my keyboard dreaming of something bigger. Over time I was rewarded for my hard work. I made first chair in our high school jazz band; I was playing at school concerts and even writing my own music. But after a while the momentum faded.

I don't know why the momentum faded. I don't know if it just got to be too hard to compete with fellow musicians. I don't know if the critique from my piano teacher felt too personal. Perhaps other passions and aspirations simply took over. All I know is that what was once a lifelong dream became nothing more than a hobby.

With the end of one dream soon came another. While I no longer had aspirations of being a famous musician, I still loved music. I started looking at other ways to share that and then I found radio. I loved the idea of connecting with people over the airwaves. I decided to pursue this in college by studying communications with a focus in radio. I loved learning the magic of mixing audio, recording artists, and producing a show. The more I learned the more I imagined myself sitting behind a board providing people with beautiful sounds.

And then one day one of my professors, a man I respected, told our class, "Radio is a dying industry; you might want to consider getting out." We asked why, and he told us that with the creation of satellite music such as Sirius/XM, there would be fewer and fewer jobs. I believed him and decided that it wasn't worth the risk, so I went back to the drawing board.

This pattern of picking a major and then finding a dead end would repeat itself over and over again in my life. You would have thought that I was indecisive, and there is some truth to that, but the reality is I didn't know who I wanted to be. I was a young man in search of his legacy, trying to figure out how he would make his mark. Never did I think it would be in youth ministry.

Taking a job in youth ministry was an accident. My original intentions, as with most youth ministers, were to work at a church for a few years until I figured out what I was *really* supposed to do for the rest of my life. Today, that's completely changed. Not only do I love youth ministry but also I embrace the challenges and constantly look at ways of growing. I eventually knew youth ministry was where God wanted me because I started to learn more about myself and how I was shaped. I finally started to discover the vision of who I was supposed to be.

Not knowing what you are supposed to *do* in life can be frustrating. However, it's not nearly as frustrating as knowing who you are supposed to *be*. Teenagers are constantly trying to figure that out. The reason they engage in a variety of activities and sports is that they are searching for their identities. They try different things and probe crucial questions about who they are and what their lives are to be about.

WHO ARE THEY SUPPOSED TO BE?

The Church has a vital role to play in helping our young people start to answer this question. Sadly, we aren't often asking them this question. Too often we instead ask them, "What do you want to do?" or "What are you going to study?" But, asking them, "Who do you want to be?" is a deeper question that forces them to think about who God has created them to be.

Confirmation preparation is the perfect time to explore this question. During this process, we are preparing them to be disciples of Jesus Christ. It's a time where they are reflecting and learning what God wants them to do with the rest of their lives.

The first time our mentors sit down with their candidates we have them ask that question, "Who do you want to be?" Most times they get blank responses, and that's because the candidates have never heard the question before. In fact, we have the mentors revisit that question throughout the process, and we want candidates to answer it with a personal vision statement. To develop a personal vision statement you need to know where you are starting. We help the candidates with their first steps in three ways.

DISCUSSING THE ANSWERS TO THEIR ESSAY QUESTIONS

In chapter 3 we looked at the five-hundred-word essay we ask each candidate to write. In the essay they need to answer one of the following two questions: *What type of Christian man or woman do you envision being in your future? What steps do you need to take to get closer to God?*

When we ask these questions we begin to learn more about their understanding of discipleship. These questions allow us to see how closely they connect to the definition of discipleship. Teenagers that identify themselves as having a relationship with Jesus Christ will tend to use personal examples. When mentors receive their candidate's application they will use the answer to these questions as a starting point for the discussion around the candidate's identity.

DIGGING INTO PSALM 139

King David wrote Psalm 139 to share the omnipresence of God. We use this verse because it shows the candidates how well God knows them. In this psalm David tells God,

> You know when I sit and stand;
> you understand my thoughts from afar. . . .
> Even before a word is on my tongue,
> LORD, you know it all. . . .
> You formed my inmost being;
> you knit me in my mother's womb.
> —Psalm 139:2, 4, 13

David continues to praise God for all the great things he does and in the end tells him,

> I praise you, because I am wonderfully made;
> wonderful are your works!
> —Psalm 139:14

Our hope is that by sharing this verse with the candidates they will see that God created them for a purpose. If they see they are wonderfully made, then they will start to see God as the answer to who they are supposed to be.

REFLECTING ON THE CAMPGROUND DRAWING

Some teenagers need a visual to help them think about their relationship with God. To help them do this we took an idea from the Alpha Youth Film Series. In episode 4, "Faith: How Can I Have

Faith?" they give participants a drawing of a public pool with a variety of characters interacting with the pool. They then pose the question: "If the water in the picture of the swimming pool represents a relationship with God, which person in the picture represents where you are?"

To fit our audience we adapted the drawing and ask a similar question: "If the campground in the picture represents your relationship with God, which person do you relate to the most?"

Looking at the campground drawing is a similar strategy to what we ask them in the application process; however, this gives them a new perspective, a fresh tool. Our hope is that the drawing will inspire a new conversation.

Once you get the candidates thinking about their current relationship with God and the Church, you can start discussing ways it can improve. This is where we introduce them to the idea of the personal vision statement. Again, to come up with one from scratch might seem impossible, so to help them we start by providing simple directions.

First, they look at what they value. On a sheet of paper we have the candidates write out a list of five to ten things they consider important. This list can be anything from relationships to objects and even experiences. The purpose of this exercise is to help them see what is important and create a conversation about which comes first.

Most times we see family and education. Candidates will share with us qualities and characteristics they think are important. They will also list the relationships they have with God, their faith, and even the local church. We want them to be open and honest. We tell them the list could be endless but that it's important to think about their top ten. We also let them know this list can change because the seasons of life change.

We ask, "Do you think these are the right values to have?" Often the candidates are confident in their answers. We then ask, "How do you know?" The reason we ask the follow-up question is to challenge their thinking and how they came to those answers.

It's not just about them having a list of values; it's also making sure they are on the right track. We ask them to probe whether what they value matches what God values for them. Most, if not all, of the values a candidate will pick are rooted in God. We ask them, "Are these the right values?" because we want them to determine the source of influence. Are their values influenced by the world or influenced by a relationship with God? Initially they might not know the answer, but throughout the Confirmation process we want them to figure that out.

Throughout the Confirmation process we have them revisit these values. As they start to grow more comfortable with scripture, we ask them to find these values in the Bible. Our hope is that they can be more confident about their God-given values because they know they are from him.

We want them to not only name their values but also own them. When you embrace a value it encourages you to work toward it. To help our candidates move from naming to owning a value, we ask them to write it into an "I" statement. For example, if they value *authenticity*, we ask them to write it out like this: "I am a man (or woman) of authenticity." Then we have them go into further detail of what that means. For example, a candidate may write,

> I am a man of authenticity. I speak words of truth. I never back away from the light. My actions and words reflect my heart, which has been given to God. I am proud of who I am, but I never let pride take control. I am blessed with how God has made me. I never try to deceive others into believing that I'm anything less or more than what God has made.

Then we have them revisit the scripture that connects it with God. A final product might look something like this:

> I am a man of authenticity. I speak words of truth. I never back away from the light. My actions and words reflect my heart, which has been given to God. I am proud of who I am, but I never let pride take control. I am blessed with how God has made me, and I never try to deceive others into believing I'm anything less or more than what God has made. 1 Samuel 16:7: "God does not see as a mortal, who sees the appearance. The LORD looks into the heart." Psalm 139:1: "LORD, you have probed me, you know me."

To be honest, most students struggle to reach this point by the end of Confirmation preparation; however, our goal is to give them that vision. That's why we tell them that this exercise should be seen as a work in progress.

A WORK IN PROGRESS

We don't have only the candidates work on personal vision statements; the mentors do as well. We want to show the candidates that this isn't just a Confirmation "thing" but a lifelong discipline.

This is something to revisit on a regular basis. I share with my candidates that I review my statement at least twice a year, on my birthday and on New Year's Day. If a major life event happens, I go to it and ask myself, *Is this what I still value?* and, *Is this what God is calling me to do?*

We want the candidates to know that being a disciple of Christ means you are constantly growing. While the plans that God has for you never change because they are more about who you become than what you do, how we perceive and understand God's desires for us will definitely change. By helping them develop a personal vision statement, you give youth an opportunity to see their faith formation as a journey. You give them the answer to the question, "Why does this all matter?"

No matter what curriculum or system you use for your Confirmation preparation, it's important to ask your candidates the question, "Who do you want to be?" It will challenge them to look deeper at themselves and to start looking closely at who God wants them to be.

Part III

S.T.E.P.S. FOR GROWING DISCIPLES

7
SERVE: GROWING ACTIVE DISCIPLES

I give you a new commandment: love one another. As I have loved you, so you also should love one another. This is how all will know that you are my disciples, if you have love for one another.

—John 13:34–35

God has called us to love others, as we would like to be loved. A growing disciple is someone who is active in his or her faith. At Church of the Nativity we believe that's done by serving in ministry and mission. When candidates learn to love others just as Jesus loved us, they will not only impact lives but also change their own.

Traffic in the Baltimore–Washington corridor is always horrible, let alone right in the middle of rush hour. But there we were, driving from the north side to the south side one day after school. I had desperately wanted to get the high school guys I was leading to serve outside the church so they could experience serving others in a new way, so we went to Sarah's House, an organization that helps homeless families in Anne Arundel County, Maryland. We were going to spend time with the kids in those families.

Despite the traffic, the day was awesome. Walking into the building, the high school guys were greeted by the little kids as if they were gods. That's because these kids knew we were there to give them our undivided time and attention. We had a blast playing basketball and Uno and eating ice-cream sundaes. But what made the day really special was the willingness of our students to serve. They weren't there to complete an obligation or fill out a time sheet. They wanted to serve—they just didn't know how until we showed them.

Serving is an important part of a disciple's journey. It challenges us to go outside our comfort zone and love others who might be different from us. The next generation wants to serve. They want to be a part of something big, and that's why you see them get emotionally charged when injustice is happening in the world.

The challenge they face is knowing where and how to make that difference. As parish communities we need to be able to provide those opportunities, and the first step is to make it not a requirement but an opportunity.

Jesus never said, "Go and make disciples for twenty hours over the course of ten months and consider yourself my friends." That would be absurd. The Bible never said anything about helping a certain amount of lepers, prostitutes, and tax collectors and that would get you into heaven. There is no minimum requirement to how much you should serve and love others.

Confirmation is the perfect place to enlighten teenagers on the spiritual habit of serving. To make Confirmation preparation tangible we throw in requirements such as service hours. It looks great when we can show others that our candidates completed a thousand, five thousand, or a million service hours. But if they aren't willing participants, it will have little or no impact on how they serve in the future.

I understand why programs require a certain amount of hours. The hope is that if teenagers give serving a try, they'll find they like it. Unfortunately, it communicates that you need to get this done and in exchange I'll give you what you want. Instead of it becoming a discipleship tool, it becomes a consumerist exchange.

We serve because Jesus wanted us to love one another in the way that he loved us. He did that by putting others first. He did that by giving his time to people who were ignored or forgotten.

Confirmation programs need to get rid of the hour requirement and start focusing on cultivating opportunities where teens can learn to love others. To cultivate those opportunities you need to start by identifying the ways that you can serve others.

There could be many others, but at Church of the Nativity we've identified two different ways.

Ministry

Ministry is serving inside the church building. When you serve in a ministry you are creating an irresistible environment for people to let down their guard and grow as disciples. Ministry helps the church staff create opportunities where people can be introduced into a personal and authentic relationship with Jesus Christ. Ministry is the way we can teach the next generation to be fully active members of the local church.

Church of the Nativity has several ministry opportunities for teenagers and adults. These opportunities range anywhere from working with kids to managing tech systems during our Mass. We have candidates serving alongside of adults opening doors, serving coffee, and helping us set up chairs for the weekend.

We want our candidates engaging in ministry opportunities so they will know what it's like to invest their time in the local church. Our hope is that after preparation for the sacrament, they will continue to participate in ministry. And we find that most teens do.

Missions

The other way we identify serving is through missions. Mission work is serving outside the church building by spreading God's love. It's going beyond our zip code and connecting with people who are very different from us. That might mean going to inner-city Baltimore, getting in a van headed to the Appalachian Mountains, or hopping on a plane to Haiti.

By serving in a mission opportunity, teenagers are stepping outside their comfort zone. They are learning more about how God has blessed them and how they do not need what the world offers to be happy. It's through our mission opportunities that teens start to change their minds about faith and life.

To get teens plugged into mission opportunities we go beyond making casseroles and building homes. We look at plugging them into a relationship with one of our strategic partners.

What's a strategic partner? It's an organization, service, or program that provides education and opportunities that will help parishioners love others and fight injustice. We currently have about a dozen strategic partners locally in Baltimore, nationally in Appalachia, and internationally in Haiti, Nigeria, and Kenya. As in ministry, we ask the teenagers to engage in missions alongside adults. That means following the vision and direction Brian Crook, our director of missions, has set forth. He is responsible for making sure we as a church are supporting those partnerships both financially and with volunteers.

There are two reasons it's important for our Confirmation team to work with Brian. The first is because finding mission opportunities for teenagers can be challenging. Unfortunately there are certain limits regarding age requirements. Brian is looking at opportunities for not only adults to serve but families as well. Partnering with him takes a lot off our plate.

The second reason is because we want the next generation learning from our generation. While teen-specific opportunities can create community, having teenagers serve alongside of adults gives them a picture of what they can do when they are older.

In the end it's about not just finding a place to serve but finding the right place. We want our candidates to learn that serving in the community, country, or around the world is more than completing a project; it's about building relationships. We partner with groups such as these because we feel God has called us to grow with them.

MOBILIZING YOUR CANDIDATES

If your parish already has a process for plugging adults into ministry and missions, just have the candidate follow the same protocol. If you don't, my suggestion is to do the following.

Create an Apprenticeship Program

Find adults who are active in your parish and ask them about taking on an apprentice. Not only will that help the candidate plug into your ministry, but also it will give another adult the opportunity to invest in the next generation.

Be careful not to have the adult just show the candidate how to do the task. Encourage them to talk about the meaning and the purpose. Show them why it matters how they set up for Mass or get ready to serve in a homeless shelter.

With an apprenticeship approach you are making it more than just a requirement; you are showing the candidate what it looks like to be an active disciple.

Help Them Find the Right Opportunity

Serving will help them to not only love others but also discover their purpose in life. That's why it's important to find the right opportunity for them to serve. To do that you need to make sure they commit to a series of genuine attempts.

Our candidates go through the same process as everyone else in the parish. We believe someone needs to try a certain serving opportunity three times before they can determine whether or not it is the right fit for them. At the end of those three trials we ask, "Do you want to keep on going or try something else?"

If they don't feel the connection we challenge them to look in a different area. If it seems as if nothing matches their personality, then assist them in discovering a new opportunity or need.

This might create a little more work, but the investment the mentor makes in helping a candidate discover where God wants them to serve is priceless. You are giving them ownership of the situation and encouraging them to go outside their comfort zone. In the end you will grow leaders that not only love to serve but also have the ability to solve problems.

Remind Them Why It Matters

Serving on a regular basis is difficult for a variety of reasons. Candidates (like everyone else) will face schedule conflicts and time restraints. Excuses will grow more tempting. They might have a negative experience during their first attempt and feel they have failed.

Mentors will help candidates navigate through the situation and remind them that growing as a disciple is a journey. Have your mentors follow up after a candidate plugs into a serving opportunity. Encourage them to connect with the adults who are apprenticing the candidate. Remind the candidates that they are not alone in the journey.

Show Them They Are Built to Serve

Serving is a spiritual discipline because God asked us and designed us to love others. To embrace this step in their faith journey you need to help teens find that identity within themselves.

To help you do this you can look at personality tests such as StrengthsFinder 2.0, Myers-Briggs, or the Birkman Method. Unfortunately, all those tests can be expensive, so we created a simple resource called GPS (Gifts, Passion, and Self). (See appendix B.)

GPS is a simple tool that helps teenagers discern where God wants them to serve. It's not as comprehensive as some of the ones I just mentioned; however, its purpose is to get the candidates thinking about God's design for them. The mentor will walk through the exercise and ask questions such as

- What talents or gifts do you possess?
- Whom do you like socializing with?
- Do you consider yourself outgoing or reserved?

These are simple questions designed to get the conversation going. After the candidate completes the exercise, our hope is that the mentor engages in a conversation focusing on where they feel called to serve and why.

Is the GPS system perfect? No, but it helps teenagers engage in a conversation about serving. In the end we want to make sure teens know why God tells us to love others. Our hope is that teenagers see that the more they put others first, the more they will discover God's blessings.

Pope Francis writes,

> What counts above all else is "faith working through love" (Gal 5:6). Works of love directed to one's neighbor are the most perfect external manifestation of the interior grace of the Spirit: "The foundation of the New Law is in the grace of the Holy Spirit, who is manifested in the faith which works through love."
>
> —*Evangelii Gaudium*, 37

Don't we want that for the next generation? Don't we want them to feel the Spirit as they serve others with love? Get rid of the requirement, walk with them on this path, and help them discover the blessing of putting their faith into action.

8
TITHE: GROWING TRUSTWORTHY DISCIPLES

Bring the whole tithe
into the storehouse,
That there may be food in my house.
Put me to the test, says the Lord of hosts,
And see if I do not open the floodgates of heaven for you,
and pour down upon you blessing without measure!

—Malachi 3:10

God wants us to trust him, and one of the best ways we can do that is through our finances. If you trust and honor God with your money, he promises to bless you beyond belief. Confirmation preparation shouldn't be the first time you talk to your teens about giving; it's a topic that should be addressed early on with elementary-age children. In Confirmation preparation you need to stress the impact tithing can have in their life. If candidates learn to manage their money wisely, they'll learn how to trust God in new and amazing ways.

I remember being jealous of my sisters every time they got to drop my parents' giving envelope in the basket. I'm not sure why I cared so much. Maybe it's because Mass was boring, and here was an opportunity to participate. It was a chance to move without getting a look from some disapproving parishioner.

As I grew older I began to understand that tangible side of giving. Each week my parents were giving money to help the church function. But how it helped the church function was a mystery. Did it go toward fixing the roof or building the new gym? What was the point of giving to the church? Didn't priests work for free? I could make assumptions; however, the point of giving didn't become clear until I actually started working for Church of the Nativity.

My wife was pregnant with our first child, Matthew. As with any expectant parents, we were neurotically going through the list of things to do such as childproofing the kitchen, buying the best bottles, and stocking up on enough diapers to absorb the Pacific Ocean. We were prepared, or at least that's what we believed, and then one day out of nowhere disaster struck. Our car started to hemorrhage oil, and our transportation budget took a huge hit. Because we were expecting our first child, our budget was limited, but we needed a car instantly.

We looked at our budget, but there was no wiggle room, and then we looked at our giving. We thought, "Well, maybe if we give a little less to the church this will help us save." The idea sounded prudent and wise; however, before we pulled the trigger, the homily that weekend dealt with trusting God with our finances. If there was ever a message from God to trust him, there it was. After much prayer and consideration we decided not to touch our giving; in fact, we increased it and said, "God, we trust you."

The next day one of my volunteers approached me and said, "Chris, we know you need a car; feel free to borrow ours for the week." At first we considered it a nice gesture from someone who was aware of our situation. But then things got a little weird.

After that week was up, someone else stepped up and let us borrow their car and then more people offered their cars. Even our pastor, Father White, allowed me, the youth minister, to borrow his only car. We started to see that in this time of need God was providing us with the margin we needed so we could save up for a new car. Finally, a good friend approached us and said, "Chris, our daughter just went away for college, and she's not going to be back for a while. Have our extra car until you can save up for a new one."

God was blessing us abundantly. On top of the accessibility to cars, we received money through different gifts and discovered savings bonds we had never seen before. It was almost as if God was saying, "See guys, I told you I had your back."

TEACHING GOD AND MONEY

When it comes to this step in our Confirmation preparation, I believe it's the most difficult one to explain to the candidates because they might wonder, "Why does God want our money?" It's not as if he's short on cash and needs a few dollars to tip the pizza guy. Or maybe he lost a bet against one of the angels. Maybe he is saving for a new smartphone or a vacation to Australia. Why would God, the Creator of the universe, need our money?

He doesn't, and neither do we. God wants us to give it away because he wants us to trust him more than anything else, and money is one of the biggest obstacles holding us back from truly trusting him. God knows it's one of the biggest obstacles to loving him. St. Paul tells St. Timothy, "For the love of money is the root of all evils, and some people in their desire for it have strayed from the faith and have pierced themselves with many pains" (1 Tm 6:10).

Now, Paul isn't saying that money is evil. It's not as if the money in your wallet is waiting for you to fall asleep to eat you alive. It's the *love* of money that hurts us. When we love money it leaves us empty, but God promises us the complete opposite.

God will not only give us what we need but also spoil us without measure (see Mal 3:10). I love this verse because I can imagine Malachi shouting these words. It's almost as if God is pounding his chest, daring us, "You don't believe me; then I triple dog dare you to test me on this."

I'm sure the Israelites hearing this were whispering, "Did he just say what I think he said?" And that's because it's contrary to what we are taught. We are taught not to test God.

According to Christian financial expert Howard Dayton, the Bible references money and possessions 2,350 times. That's insane. That means God thinks what we own and how we manage our money matters. Yet when do we ever talk about it in our Confirmation process?

I'm willing to bet we don't. When I was researching other Confirmation-preparation programs for this book, I didn't find any mention of money management. And that's a shame because God is constantly warning us about storing up earthly treasures. He is constantly telling people how hard it is to enter the kingdom of heaven if you can't let go of your riches. In the *Catechism* it says, "Detachment from riches is necessary for entering the Kingdom of heaven. 'Blessed are the poor in spirit'" (*CCC*, 2556). And one of the best ways to detach yourself from your money and belongings is by learning how to give it away. That's where tithing and worship offerings are key. Before I start talking about how we help candidates build this discipline, I think it's important for us to define tithing.

Tithe Means 10 Percent

I've heard many different interpretations of this word. I've heard people say they tithe 2 percent or 8 percent. Or people say, "Well I tithe because half goes to serving and the rest is giving."

Last time I checked, *to tithe* means to give 10 percent of annual produce or earnings. I googled it and looked it up in the dictionary, and it pretty much means 10 percent.

Tithing is a habit, and it should be done consistently; anything spontaneous or in addition to it is a worship offering. A worship offering is something you might feel compelled to do because of a certain cause.

God is asking us to tithe, and whether you're a broke teenager or a multimillionaire, giving 10 percent right off the bat is difficult. Knowing that teenagers might perceive 10 percent as a big jump, we help them build this step by understanding their finances better.

Getting to Know Their Financial IQ

I love asking the candidates to estimate the cost of certain items such as cars and mattresses. Most of the answers are uneducated, which leads to some interesting responses. I've had teens tell me that a house will cost $3,000 and a car could be $200,000.

The teens' answers are all over the place, but you can't blame them. Their financial responsibilities are minimal, and the risks are low. Their parents provide most of their everyday needs, and they don't have to buy anything of huge value such as a car or a house.

We've learned that the first time teenagers in our community really start looking at money is when their parents start talking to them about college. Even then, the conversation is more about the type of loan they will take out and not how to avoid graduating hundreds of thousands of dollars in debt.

To help a candidate take that first step, you need to be able to get them thinking about money. Start with a simple conversation, and get to know what they know, who taught it to them, and what they think about money.

Give Them Basic Money-Management Tools

Each of our mentors is given a budget sheet to go through with the candidate. A budget sheet is one of the most simple yet impactful tools you can give a teenager. We show them that even though they have very little money, they should start tracking it because the Bible says, "The person who is trustworthy in very small matters is also trustworthy in great ones; and the person who is dishonest in very small matters is also dishonest in great ones" (Lk 16:10).

We don't need to start talking to them about 401(k)s and Roth IRAs, but we do want them developing a plan where they are giving, saving, and spending wisely. We then want them to take that conversation home and talk to their parents about money.

To accomplish this we have them fill out a budget sheet with their parents. It's during times such as this that we discover parents also need assistance with their relationship with money.

As a church we help teenagers with their finances by offering Dave Ramsey's course "Generation Change (Financial Peace University for Adults)." "Generation Change" is a nine-week course where teenagers learn not only how to manage money but also how to use it in a God-honoring way. We offer this course to all of our teenagers; however, we especially encourage Confirmation candidates to take it.

In the end, if we are helping these candidates win with their money then we are helping them win with their relationship with God. Confident money managers become confident givers, and that's why we need to give them the tools they need to do so.

Provide Opportunities to Give

Tithing is a spiritual habit we start teaching in early childhood. Kids get an opportunity to give during Time Travelers, our children's Liturgy of the Word program. As they get older we invite them to give at Mass or at our student programs, Resurrection (middle school) and Uprising (high school).

And then there are our church-wide giving initiatives. Each year around Advent we'll have a weekend where we encourage our congregation to give toward a missions project. The projects have ranged from building wells in Nigeria to creating a lunch program with our sister parish in Haiti. We want teenagers to find opportunities where they learn to tithe and give with Christ in mind.

The more they embrace this step, the more it's going to set them up for a healthier relationship with money and God. By giving to God first, we will help them learn to trust him. And not only will they trust God but also they will open themselves up to his blessings.

I love what Pope Francis says in *Evangelii Gaudium*, 58:

> Money must serve, not rule! The pope loves everyone, rich and poor alike, but he is obliged in the name of Christ to remind all that the rich must help, respect and promote the poor. I exhort you to generous solidarity and to the return of economics and finance to an ethical approach which favours human beings.

Money must serve, not rule! Imagine the next generation embracing that statement. Imagine if teens learned through healthy money practices to trust God. You would not only commission a stronger generation of disciples but also build a healthier church culture.

9

ENGAGE: GROWING RELATIONAL DISCIPLES

I, then, a prisoner for the Lord, urge you to live in a manner worthy of the call you have received, with all humility and gentleness, with patience, bearing with one another through love, striving to preserve the unity of the spirit through the bond of peace.

—Ephesians 4:1–3

We are not meant to get through life on our own. God shows his love by surrounding us with people who hold us accountable to grow in our faith. Confirmation preparation is the perfect time to help a candidate reflect on the relationships he or she is building. On top of mentoring, we want to make sure the candidate is connecting in Christlike relationships.

One of my favorite parts of Confirmation preparation is reading the letters that we have candidates write to the bishop. In most letters you'll find the candidates praising their mentors for the time and energy they spent over the last year walking with them in faith. But it's especially awesome when they talk about other relationships they have. A few years ago we received this letter from one of our candidates:

Dear Bishop,
    Over the past year I have found and seen a change in myself and how I am as a Catholic. My faith has strengthened

in many different aspects. This time last year I had fallen into depression and had lost hope in a lot, mainly God. I lost most my faith and claimed I didn't believe in God because I couldn't understand why he created life and took it away, why the culture I live in didn't support the Catholic culture, and how it was possible for God to work with and in me. I was growing up and had doubts in my faith. Even though I went to therapy I still felt like something [was] missing.

One of my best friends, Allie, works at Nativity and loves it. She seemed so sure of herself, and I looked up to her. One day she and I were talking about Confirmation; she was signing up and wanted me to join to show me what I was missing. After more discussion I decided to join in on the Confirmation process. Allie also invited me to join her small group to show me how being surrounded with other Catholics may help fill that void inside of me. I joined and later that year I slowly found myself enjoying the church atmosphere. Being with others who shared my Catholic faith helped me immensely. I now feel proud to say I'm a Catholic and that I believe in God. I go almost every Thursday night to youth group, and I go to church every Sunday with my parents.

In addition to Allie, my mentor, Kate, helped me focus and understand God better. She and I met every month through the Confirmation process, and together we worked on building spiritual habits. She helped me look at the talents I have and showed me that God gave me the ability to understand and listen. She showed me that I could use those gifts to brighten and impact someone's day.

Allie and Kate are the main reasons I am devoted to live like God and Jesus and the reason I go to church and youth group; they both showed me the missing piece in my life, and I never want to lose it. I was able to find my whole self and I want to grow more in church in my faith. I want to thank the two of them and the Church of the Nativity for guiding me and making my life whole again. This Confirmation process has taken me on the journey that I cannot wait for others to enjoy.

There are so many moments to celebrate in this letter, and they all link back to one thing: *relationships*. Because of the relationships this candidate formed with her friend, mentor, and small group, her faith grew and her life began to change. When someone discovers the power of Christ-centered relationships, they will begin to recognize that faith involves a loving community.

In chapter 4 we spent some time looking at the importance of moving away from the classroom feel. This testimonial letter drives home that point even further. If we continue to treat faith as a class, then the next generation will continue to miss out on the joys that relational ministry can bring. God created us to have relationships; that's why he said, "It is not good for the man to be alone. I will make a helper suited to him" (Gn 2:18).

Our Confirmation program is the perfect opportunity to connect the next generation into relationships that will encourage them to grow in their faith in many different ways. While mentoring is the backbone to our Confirmation preparation, we also want to connect our candidates into Christ-centered relationships through intergenerational ministry and small groups.

INTERGENERATIONAL MINISTRY

In chapter 7 we discussed the importance of serving in ministry and mission. Not only does it give our candidates an opportunity to love God and love others but it also introduces them to men and women who are active in their faith. A teenager might initially get involved with a certain ministry because the task is what interests them. But over time they begin to realize that growing in one's faith is more than just personal prayer. By serving with others they begin to see that community is essential to learning more about God as we see in part of this candidate's letter:

The tech ministry at my church is 100 percent volunteer members; we operate cameras, lighting, music and sound during the Mass. We are the iconic "12th" man of the Church of the Nativity. Working with all my co-worker volunteer members I have come to learn the definition of giving. These kind people show up week after week, give it their all, and don't ask for anything in return. They are the most generous people, and I love their ideals. I work on the cameras during Mass whenever they need me. I show up, try my best, and have a great time. It gives me a glimpse into the film production world every time I ready my camera and put on my headset. I am very glad that I became involved with this great program, and it has opened two different doors for me. I have now figured out that I love operating cameras and I am considering that for a career option. Being around these people has helped me realize how God shapes people into well natured human beings that put others before themselves. They are becoming the unsung heroes of our generation while trying to live their lives for God.

This candidate's faith grew because of the people serving around him. He felt he was a part of a team, which is essential for a young disciple to learn. It shows them that discipleship involves community. It shows them that the success of the Church doesn't just fall on the shoulders of the clergy and that the people who call themselves Christians share it.

To get candidates plugged into intergenerational relationships you need to do the following.

Identify Ministry Leaders Who Value the Investment

There will be men and women in your church who love their ministry but do not understand the value of investing in the next generation. That's okay; it's just where they are in their faith journey. But there are people who care so much about what they do that they are willing to share it with others, especially your candidates.

Identify these people, and bring them together to share the vision of what you are trying to do. Ask them to keep an eye out for opportunities to not only teach what they do but also to share why it impacts their faith. Once you've assembled this team, you'll know where to send your candidates to not only give them a serving experience but also another adult disciple who will invest in them further.

Connect Mentors with Ministry Leaders

Build the team of adults around your candidates by connecting the mentor with the ministry leader. Encourage them to discuss what the candidate is doing well, what they could be doing better, and ways they can share their faith.

Have the mentor share with the ministry leader what the discussion between them and the candidate looks like. The more they communicate, the more they'll be able to pour into the candidate's faith journey.

SMALL-GROUP MINISTRY

While mentoring is the backbone to our Confirmation preparation, our hope is to lead students to join a high school small group. Small groups are an essential part of our parish. It's where our big church gets intimate and personal.

What started as a program for high school students has now become a way that people receive pastoral care. It's an opportunity for people to share what is happening in their lives and go further in the message they heard on the weekend. In the book *Rebuilt*, Tom Corcoran and Father Michael White note, "The power of small groups comes from forming relationships in which conversations lead to conversion" (162).

We know that the next generation is going to be more open and confident to explore their faith if they are surrounded by accountability. Being in a small group gives teens the permission to talk about their Catholic faith without judgment. When teens feel free to share their struggles and blessings, they are allowed to build trust. It's through these relationships that teens learn to trust one another and God.

We want our candidates to engage in as many Christ-centered relationships as possible. With mentoring, they have an adult who is investing in them; small groups give them an opportunity to grow with their peers; and by serving in a ministry they learn how to work with different generations.

The more relationships we can build with them in the local parish, the more they are going to feel connected to the local parish. This is especially key for when they decide on college and move away. We believe that if they get a taste of Christian fellowship, it will influence them to seek out other Christ-like relationships. And the perfect place to find those is in a campus ministry and the local parish.

To build a small-group program I would encourage you to read my book *Rebuilding Youth Ministry*. But to get started, try the following.

Pick Authentic and Patient Adults

Small-group leaders aren't people who have it all figured out. They are people who love God, love others, and care deeply about their Catholic faith. They are men and women who understand that faith is a journey and are willing to come alongside of a teenager who is discovering that.

Recruit men and women who are great listeners. They are people who look for the emotion beneath the story. They are looking to create a community of teens who can encourage one another and hold one another accountable.

Develop a Simple Structure

Small groups should not be complicated. They are what they sound like: a small group of people who gather to share life, pray together, and grow together. Our high school groups meet weekly on Thursday, and our middle school groups meet weekly on Sunday nights. Why those nights?

Thursday works for our high school students because it's toward the end of the week and they have gotten into the rhythm of work practices and are feeling more relaxed because of the upcoming weekend. Our high school groups meet after 7:00 p.m. because it gives them enough time to go home and get changed if they are playing a sport.

Our middle school small groups meet Sunday nights because there are fewer conflicts for the teens and their parents who have to drive them. We start our groups after 6:30 p.m. so they can still have dinner with their families and not get home too late on a school night.

Each group has about six to eight students with two adult leaders. They are divided by age and gender. While you can have mixed groups, we desire focused discussion, and sometimes mixed groups can cause too many distractions.

Start Slowly

While our groups meet weekly, they started out just meeting for six weeks in the fall and six weeks during Lent. Doing a six-week series was easier to commit to for the students and the leaders. Over time the impact grew and so did the desire to keep meeting. Now our groups meet from September to May on a regular basis.

If you are going to improve your Confirmation preparation, you need to consider the programs and ministries that surround it. Intergenerational ministry and small groups should be continuous and offered to everyone in the parish. Our hope is that eventually all teenagers are already participating in these programs before they enter preparation. Our thought is that if a student already knows how to grow with others, their experience of sacramental prep will be that much deeper.

Instead of going through Confirmation preparation isolated, they will now have a community that supports them. They will see that faith is not private but something to be shared and celebrated with others. Before you revamp your entire Confirmation preparation program, I would suggest you look at the other ways you plug students into parish relationships. The more you plug them into these relationships, the more connected they will feel to the local church. The more they feel connected to the local church, the more likely it is they will know what to look for when they move onto the next chapter of their life.

10
PRACTICE: GROWING DEEPER DISCIPLES

In praying, do not babble like the pagans, who think that they will be heard because of their many words. Do not be like them. Your Father knows what you need before you ask him.

—Matthew 6:7–8

Prayer is a conversation with God. Unfortunately, students engaging in the sacraments aren't sure how to start that conversation. During our Confirmation process we give them the tools to practice their faith through prayer, scripture, and sacramental life. When they have tools they'll start to see their faith more as a relationship and less as a set of rules.

I love the movie *Meet the Parents* starring Ben Stiller and Robert De Niro. Stiller plays a guy who is in love, and he's meeting the girl's parents for the first time in the hope of receiving their blessing for marriage. Throughout the movie there are situations where Greg (Stiller) is doing everything to impress Jack (De Niro). My favorite scene is when Jack asks Greg to say the prayer before dinner. Nervously he agrees and says,

> O dear God, thank you.
> You are such a good God to us.
> A kind and gentle and accommodating God.
> And we thank you O sweet, sweet Lord of hosts for the smorgasbord

you have so aptly lain at our table this day, and each
day . . . by day.
Day by day, by day. O dear Lord, three things we pray:
To love thee more dearly, to see thee more clearly,
to follow thee more nearly day by day. By day.
Amen.

Unfortunately, we find candidates who struggle to start a conversation with God. It can be humorous to listen to and frustrating to work with. What lacks isn't just knowledge; it's also a lack of confidence. Anytime I ask candidates that I'm mentoring to pray, it's almost as if I've asked them to stand up on their chair in the middle of a busy restaurant and proclaim, "I love SpongeBob SquarePants!"

It's a challenge because we're told so many things about practicing our faith. We're told it needs to be done like *this*, while doing *this*, and you have to hold *this* and think about *this*. Sometimes I think flying a rocket ship would be easier.

Practicing our faith should not be complicated; it should not feel like a set of rules or else we risk being like the Pharisees that Jesus called out in the Bible: "Woe to you, scribes and Pharisees, you hypocrites. You are like whitewashed tombs, which appear beautiful on the outside, but inside are full of dead men's bones and every kind of filth" (Mt 23:27).

The fourth step we want all of our candidates to learn is how to practice their faith through prayer, scripture, and sacraments. Granted there are several other ways to practice our faith, and some of them we've already covered, but we broke it down to these three sections because we felt that prayer, scripture, and sacraments were a way to get to know God personally. St. Isidore of Seville informs us, "Prayer purifies us, reading instructs us. . . . If a man wants to be always in God's company, he must pray regularly and read regularly. When we pray, we talk to God; when we read, God talks to us" (CatholicSaints.Info). The bottom line is, we want candidates to know how to build a personal and authentic relationship with Jesus Christ.

PRACTICE PRAYER

Prayer is a conversation with God. For a long time I thought it was how we talked to God, but the reality is that it's a conversation. It's learning how to not only speak to him but listen as well. And some people know this; however, we get focused on talking a certain way or looking out for specific signs. When our expectations are not met, we grow disappointed. We want our candidates to avoid setting false expectations. We want them to understand that God communicates to us in a variety of ways.

Explaining to them how God communicates or responds to us is important. Many times they'll wonder, *Why can't I hear God as people thousands of years ago could?* And the truth is that they aren't recognizing his promptings and voice. Instead of teaching students different types of prayers, we need to show them how to pray. In fact, that's what Christ did when he taught the disciples.

So how do we do that? We ask our mentors to guide them through exercises where we take several stories from scripture that describe various encounters with God. The readings we use are:

- Exodus 18:5–26: Moses Encounters the Burning Bush
  God communicates with to us through signs
- Judges 6:12–25, 36–40: The Angel Appearing to Gideon
  God uses messengers to share his plan
- 1 Kings 19:11–18: The Lord Appears to Elijah
  God is found in the stillness of a crazy world
- 1 Samuel 3: The Lord Calls Samuel
  Recognizing God's voice for the first time
- Acts 10:1–23: Cornelius Calls Peter
  God uses dreams to speak to his people

Are they the only encounters God has with people? No. Are these the only ways God will speak to us? Of course not. Exploring these scripture readings simply gets the ball rolling. We want our candidates to consider that maybe they had a misperception when it comes to knowing how God wants to speak to us.

After mentor and candidate choose one of the readings, they then reflect on them using the following questions: *Who is talking with God? How did God communicate with them? What did God say? How did they react?*

By looking at others we hope our students start to see how God can interact with us. Again, to cover every single way God works in and around our lives would be impossible, so we just pick a few.

After the mentor and candidate complete this exercise, they begin discussing how to apply what they've learned. This is where the mentor shares personal prayer habits with the candidates. We have some who are into the rosary and others who share the Liturgy of the Hours or just quiet-time devotionals. The mentor can really help that candidate understand the many different ways God communicates with us by showing them the endless amount of tools and resources for personal prayer available.

PRACTICE SCRIPTURE

Growing up my family had a complete *Encyclopedia Britannica* set. As a kid I loved learning about dinosaurs, exploring outer space, and getting to know all about World War II. To navigate through the collection you had to know how to search through a glossary and what the different volumes, chapters, and page numbers meant. There was a learning process, but once you knew it there was no problem.

Knowing how to navigate through scripture is essential. The more comfortable you are at understanding the difference between chapters and verses, Old and New Testaments, gospels and epistles, and the prophets and the law, the more likely it is you are going to read the Bible.

In fact, many people forget that the Bible is a collection of books, written by different people at different times and for different reasons. Not only is the Bible put together differently than any other piece of literature our teenagers come across but also it's to be read differently. I know to the average Christian I might be stating the obvious, but assuming that the next generation understands this right away is a huge mistake.

The first step to getting candidates comfortable with scripture is introducing them to verses that will capture their interests. While we could make them memorize key verses, we use an ancient tradition to help them see scripture as more than words. Each of our mentors lead their mentees through an exercise called *lectio divina* (Latin for "divine reading"). This is a traditional practice of scripture reading, meditation, and prayer intended to bring one into communion with God. It does not treat scripture as texts to be studied but as the Living Word of God.

While there are different approaches to this ancient tradition, we give our mentors these directions:

- *Step 1*: Choose a text of the scriptures that you wish to pray with the candidate. When choosing scripture, length of text can all depend on what God is calling you to do; it can be a verse or an entire chapter. With the candidates, something brief is best.
- *Step 2*: Place yourself in a comfortable position, and allow yourself to become silent. Some Christians focus for a few moments on their breathing; others have a beloved "prayer word" or "prayer phrase" they gently recite. Some use the practice known as "centering prayer," which makes a good, brief introduction to lectio divina. Use whatever method is best for you, and allow yourself to enjoy silence for a few moments.
- *Step 3*: Turn to the text and read it slowly, gently. Encourage the candidate to take in each portion of the reading, constantly listening for the "still, small voice" of a word or phrase that somehow says, *I am for you today*. Let them know that the phrase or word may not jump out at them but reveal itself slowly. Have them share that word or phrase and repeat it. Do the same with the word you have taken in from the exercise.

- *Step 4*: Read the text again; however, this time ask the candidates to place themselves in the scene or in a situation where they are speaking to God. Spend some time discussing the scene or situation they envisioned while rereading the passage.
- *Step 5*: Read the text for a third time, and ask the candidate to contemplate on what God is inviting them to do. What do they think is being communicated, what is God trying to tell them, and what is revealing itself through scripture? If you and the candidate wish to reread the text again, feel free; there are unlimited amounts of time one can reflect on a passage.

Again, there are different approaches a mentor can take, and we give them this list of readings:

- Psalm 23: The Lord, Shepherd, and Host
- Matthew 7:13–14: The Narrow Gate
- Mark 4:35–41: The Calming of a Storm at Sea
- Luke 22:39–44: The Agony in the Garden
- John 15:1–17: The Vine and the Branches
- Philippians 2:1–11: Plea for Unity and Humility

As you can see, some of the readings are shorter than others. Some tell the story of Jesus and others paint a picture. When picking what readings to use we just wanted ones that would provoke different images and feelings.

A few years back on the Confirmation retreat we asked students to grab their Bibles. I was very adamant about them bringing one from home. What surprised me was the array of translations and sizes that teenagers brought. A few had brought the family Bible their parents received when they were married—you know, the coffee-table kind. One had a children's Bible they probably got at First Communion, and one student had a King James Version that was probably given to their great-grandparents. Leading those teens through the readings was a challenge because you had comments such as

- "My Bible doesn't say that."
- "My story is on a different page."
- "I don't think my Bible is in English."

When Bibles became available on smartphones and tablets, life became a little easier. You can just search a story, keyword, or verse and immediately receive what you are looking for. And while I recommend our candidates download an app, we still stress having their own personal Bible.

We want them to see scripture as something personal. We want our candidates to feel they can write in the margins, break in the binding, and build an attachment to God's Word. We guide them in the purchase of a Bible by helping them find a translation that's easy to understand and true to their Catholic faith.

We want candidates to be comfortable with scripture because we want them to know they have a source of wisdom that will help them navigate life. We want them finding comfort in God's Word when life gets crazy. The more they understand how to use the Bible, the more confident they will be growing in their faith.

PRACTICE SACRAMENTAL LIFE

For many candidates preparation for Confirmation is the first time in a long time they get to revisit any of the sacraments. While they might receive the Eucharist on Sunday, knowing what they are doing hasn't been discussed since they hit second grade. Confession was something they had to get done and over with, and maybe they went to a family member's baptism or wedding, but that was more about the cake and food at the party.

> "Seated at the right hand of the Father" and pouring out the Holy Spirit on his Body which is the Church, Christ now acts through the sacraments he instituted to communicate his grace. The sacraments are perceptible signs (words and actions) accessible to our human nature. By the action of

Christ and the power of the Holy Spirit they make present efficaciously the grace that they signify.

—*Catechism of the Catholic Church*, 1084

If we can't show the next generation how to access the sacraments, they will struggle to embrace God's grace on a regular basis. We have our mentors take candidates to confession or attend adoration before their one-on-one. We also make sure candidates and their families are aware of the confession schedule and when the diocese is hosting a vocation's event.

Honestly, we're still figuring out ways that we can connect candidates with the sacraments in new and different ways. This is an area where we encourage the mentors to share their ideas with the other mentors.

Practicing your faith sounds odd when it comes to a personal relationship with Jesus Christ. But to prepare these candidates for the next stage of their journey we need to help them see how they can reach out, listen, speak to, and embrace the grace that God is giving them. As St. Margaret Mary Alocoque said, "Until we have acquired genuine prayer, we are like people teaching children to begin to walk" (Saintsquotes.blogspot.com). If we want growing disciples who are helping others grow then we need to help them take it from a tradition to a habit and eventually to a way of life.

11
SHARE: GROWING BOLD DISCIPLES

For so the Lord has commanded us, "I have made you a light to the Gentiles, that you may be an instrument of salvation to the ends of the earth."

—Acts 13:47

Your faith is personal, but it's not meant to be private. Jesus told his disciples to go and make disciples. We prepare students to receive the sacrament of Confirmation because we want them to be confident to go out and make disciples. The problem is that going out and sharing your faith publicly can be intimidating for teenagers because they are already looking to be accepted. If they go out and say something that could be considered confrontational or even hateful, this could create alienation.

As a teenager I loved going to youth group. Every Sunday night I spent time with a group of people who loved me and supported me for who I was. Going on retreats was even better because it meant an escape from the craziness of life and a chance to form new friendships with kids that didn't go to my school.

Having this group of friends was awesome because I felt comfortable praying with them and talking about Church with them. The more I got to know them, the more I wanted to spend time with them. It was a great situation to be in until my friends from school started wondering where I was going.

It's not that my friends at school were oblivious to my faith; it's just that they didn't know how invested and involved I was. When we hung out, the conversation always centered on homework, classes, sports, and everything associated with our school. I'm sure anytime I chose my church friends over my school friends they were curious as to who these people were.

It's not that people didn't know I went to church. They knew I was Catholic; they just didn't know that three or four times a year I went away on retreat. They didn't know I had this other group of friends who went to different schools but believed the same thing I did.

Not only is sharing your faith intimidating but also somewhere and somehow we made it complicated by mixing in apologetics. We've confused sharing our faith with defending our faith. While there is a need for knowing the dogma, not everyone you need to share with is on the attack. They just want to know why it's important to you.

I'm not sure how the conversation started, but there I was getting ready for soccer practice and arguing with another student about God's existence. He was mocking me and my faith, and with each comment I grew more and more frustrated. With each ignorant comment I responded with one equally, if not more, ignorant. I was upset and irritated and didn't like what he was saying.

The problem with this tactic is that other people were watching, and whether or not they cared about who was right and who was wrong they were seeing me act as anything but a disciple of Jesus Christ. Mahatma Gandhi once said, "I like your Christ, I do not like your Christians. Your Christians are so unlike your Christ." A lot of our teenagers are facing this conflict. They like the idea of having a relationship with Jesus Christ, but to be a witness? They don't want to be associated with a name that has been tied in with Westboro Baptist Church or the Ku Klux Klan. Whenever it comes to defending their faith, all they can think of are images of people holding signs, yelling, calling people sinners, and condemning others to hell. Sharing our faith shouldn't be that complicated, but we've made it complicated, encouraging these teens to brush up on their apologetics and to be persistent in standing up against those who attack the faith.

I do think there is an attack on our faith, and I do believe there are people out there trying to snuff out Christianity, but I also know that this isn't anything new. In fact, it's all a part of the spiritual battle that's been going on since the Fall. But if we want the next generation to really *go and make disciples*, we need to help them take the next step of sharing their faith through a simple strategy called Invest and Invite.

To invest means to simply get to know the people around you. It's not about winning them over to believe what you believe, at least not right away. It's about building trust, and the way to build trust is to love them, listen to them, and get to know them as a child of God.

Once the trust is formed, you can take the conversations to a deeper and more profound level. Personal subjects such as family, fears, and faith can now be shared. When you have trust you allow God to create opportunities to invite that person to get to know more about your faith.

As a church we try to keep that simple by encouraging our members to invite people to Mass, student programs, or small groups. We want our parishioners, especially the next generation, confident in knowing that what they are inviting their friends to is something worth their while.

When it comes to the Confirmation program, we emphasize the relationship that mentors are forming with their candidates. We remind our mentors that what they are doing is investing in the next generation and inviting them to learn more about Christ through a relationship with them. We've seen the best response when our mentors, the candidates, and their families form a personal relationship. They begin to see that faith is more than a bunch of religious rules and traditions. It's about forming relationships where Christ is present and known.

To help candidates Invest and Invite we do the following.

FOCUS THEM ON THE INVESTMENT

It's easy to get hung up on the idea of spouting out truth and wanting to convert someone by the end of a conversation. Although possible, it's unlikely. We tell our candidates to think of someone they know who does not yet know Christ.

For some of them it might be a classmate or a neighbor. Sometimes it's a sibling or even a parent. We want them to pick one person they can get to know on a deeper level during this process. That might mean looking at ways to serve them and put them first. While we want them to share their faith and invite them into an opportunity where they can connect with Christ, the primary focus is relationship building.

We've found that even this can be intimidating to teenagers. Getting to know someone intentionally means making yourself vulnerable. It means thinking of yourself second, and that can feel awkward. We remind teenagers that the investment is important because it builds trust and with trust comes the opportunity to ask someone else to walk out of their comfort zone.

REASSURE THEM GOD WILL GIVE OPPORTUNITIES

Many of our candidates think of someone and are immediately excited about the idea of bringing someone to faith. The problem is they don't know how to create an opportunity to invite someone to get to know God.

We remind them that they have weekly opportunities with our high school youth program and the weekend liturgy. For many of our students it's been a simple step because those are things they've already talked to some of their friends about. But sometimes inviting them to the youth ministry or Mass is a little challenging.

This is where it's important for mentors to share their struggles and successes with inviting someone to get to know Christ. We want candidates to know that there will be times when someone says no.

Of course, no one really likes to hear the word *no*. It's a rejection that can be demoralizing, but only if you make it about yourself. We remind our candidates that when someone says no to their invitation, it's not a reflection of who they are. Asking someone to check out Mass, go to church, or talk about their faith can be scary.

While there might be trust in the relationship, what you are doing is asking them to step out of their comfort zone. To help them move past the fear of *no*, we help them find patience in the process. We tell them not to make deadlines but to commit to praying for that person.

By praying for the person, they are asking God to open up the person's heart and present an opportunity where the invitation won't seem so overwhelming. The more they can rely on God, the more they can be guided to invest and invite on a personal level.

GIVE THEM TOOLS
TO DEVELOP THEIR STORY

Invest and Invite is supposed to be a personal and authentic process; however, it's still important to prepare for these moments. To be prepared to invest and invite, you need to make sure you are confident in your own faith story.

While most of our candidates won't find themselves standing on stage at our youth program sharing their testimony, we feel it's important for them to learn it. To help them share their story we've developed this tool called Write Your Own Story.

Step 1: Sit in Prayer

Your story is a part of a bigger story; it's a part of God's story. Believe it or not, your story needs to be shared with others. Before you even start thinking about who you will tell it to or what it entails, take some time silently reflecting how God has worked in and out of your life. Here are a few questions to help you sort your thoughts:

- What's your earliest memory regarding God, religion, or faith?
- What were you told about church and God growing up?
- When did God first reveal himself to you? What was going on in your life?

- What was life before you embraced your relationship with God?
- What is your life like now that you know him?
- Why should others get to know God?

Step 2: Write It Out

One of the reasons we don't share our story is because we don't know how to do so. Even though your story is personal and intimate, if not fleshed out it becomes unexplainable. Again your story needs to be shared; therefore, here are some steps to help you construct your testimony.

- Introduction: Share with everyone your identity.
    Name
    School
    Grade
    A little background on family
    What makes you, you?
- Recognizing God: This is where you talk about faith, religion, and God.
    Part 1: Before you knew God (or when you were a child), what did you believe? Share with your peers misconceptions and understandings you had about your faith. Tell them how this perception caused problems, conflict, and frustration in your life.
    Part 2: When did your perception of God change? Share with your peers that moment, conversation, or experience that started to change the way you saw life and your relationship with him.
- How Life Has Changed: Now that God has worked through your life, relationship, or situation, how have you grown? Why are you more at peace, or how do you have more confidence in God? The reason you are sharing your story is to show someone how God fills your life. It doesn't mean everything is perfect; it just means you see everything more clearly.

Step 3: Practice It

Don't be shocked if the first time you read your story it sounds funny, odd, or even confusing. Verbalizing it is a big thing, and it needs practice. Be sure to read it to a trusted friend or family member who knows you and the story. They'll help you figure out what is missing and what needs to be revised.

Once you've written something you are content with, start memorizing it. When you memorize you take ownership and allow God to speak through you.

Write Your Own Story gives candidates the ability to think out how God has worked in their lives. It allows them to reflect on what he is doing and where he is taking them. When a candidate has this type of clarity, it builds confidence. When they have confidence, there will be more opportunities to use this story in real settings.

CELEBRATE THE WINS

One of the most frustrating parts of the Invest and Invite strategy is not knowing whether or not you've made a difference. You might hear several *nos* until you get a *maybe*. You might spend years investing in someone and not knowing if they are listening to what you have to say or if they really care.

To help our candidates through this process, we need to help them identify small successes. That's why it's important to walk through the process with them.

We had one candidate whose father did not go to church. When her mentor asked her why he didn't go, she explained, "I don't know; it's always been my mother who's brought us to church." The mentor asked her what she thought about the situation and could tell it was upsetting to the candidate.

The mentor shared with her how it can be difficult to see family members unconnected to something that means so much to you. She encouraged the candidate to pray about the situation and bring it to God. Throughout the preparation the topic came up several times. Each time they discussed the importance of being present and of the candidate sharing with her father what was going on in her faith journey.

Finally, one Sunday her mentor got a lovely surprise. She was attending Mass with her husband when she noticed the candidate was with her family, including her father. The mentor took the opportunity to say hello to the girl and her parents without making the father's attendance a spectacle. She said the girl was glowing.

When the mentor followed up and asked the candidate how she got her dad to go, the candidate responded, "It was simple; I told him I would really like him to join me, and he said he would."

It might seem like a simple step to ask family members to come to Mass, but it has such a profound impact. This girl was able to see the instant fruits of inviting someone to church, and her mentor was there to point that out.

To evangelize is challenging, but it's necessary. Without this step your candidates will only learn to grow a faith that is private. When you invest and invite others into a relationship with Jesus Christ, you do what Pope Francis hopes for in *Evangelii Gaudium*, 10:

> When the Church summons Christians to take up the task of evangelization, she is simply pointing to the source of authentic personal fulfillment. For "here we discover a profound law of reality: that life is attained and matures in the measure that it is offered up in order to give life to others. This is certainly what mission means."

When you help the next generation see that they have a story worth sharing, you help them go beyond the church walls. You allow them to see that faith is something more than just a personal belief. When you help them share that faith, you help them see how life changing God's love truly is.

CONCLUSION
HEADING IN THE RIGHT DIRECTION AND TRACKING YOUR PROGRESS

Jesus replied, "Do not prevent him. There is no one who performs a mighty deed in my name who can at the same time speak ill of me. For whoever is not against us is for us. Anyone who gives you a cup of water to drink because you belong to Christ, amen, I say to you, will surely not lose his reward."

—Mark 9:39–41

Even after all the time and energy you spend developing a program, it's easy to wonder, "Am I really making an impact?" Tracking where people are going and how they are moving is key. The challenge is measuring that progress because it means measuring life change.

One day I was sitting down with one of my volunteer leaders, and she asked the question, "Chris, how do we know if we are doing enough? I mean, are we just guessing when it comes to ministry?" It's a great question, one that haunts every youth minister as teenagers graduate from high school and head into the next season of life. It's rare when we get to witness the results of our hard work.

Recently, a former student of mine passed away. While it's not the first time I've lost a student, it was definitely the most difficult one to deal with. I had known this young man since he was a middle school student. Over the years I developed a relationship with his parents, especially his father who has become a close friend. My family became close with his family. This young man, an artist, painted a mural in our son's room. My wife had an opportunity to mentor his younger sister during her Confirmation preparation. To lose him felt like losing a member of my family.

It's during some of the most difficult times that God shows us his glory and love. The family had asked if I would lead a prayer service at the funeral home. I was nervous and honored at the same time. I love this family and wanted to show my support in any way. As I entered the funeral home that evening, I was greeted by a number of former students. Time had definitely flown by; what were once scrawny middle school students were now full-fledged adults out of college and starting a whole new chapter in life.

As we chatted many of them thanked me for the men and women who had mentored them during their time preparing for Confirmation. They shared with me specific encounters when their mentors did or said something profound. They made a point to say that the men and women who had walked with them during their high school years had impacted their faith. During one of the saddest moments of my life I received probably one of the strongest affirmations of my career.

I don't know if I'll ever receive feedback such as that again. To wait and hope for those moments will only lead to discouragement. God will bless you for the work that you do, and to appreciate it you need to set up systems and structures that will let you know you are on the right track.

Our Confirmation program has a few systems in place to help us know whether we are making a difference.

SURVEY YOUR MENTORS

At the end of each year I send a survey to mentors. I keep the survey anonymous because I don't want them to fear letting me down.

I have very loyal ministers, and I want to return that loyalty by showing them that I listen.

In the survey I ask them to evaluate the materials, the information that I provide for them, and my availability. Mentoring can be a lonely ministry, and if a mentor does not feel supported, they won't return. What I've mostly found is that a first-year mentor will critique the materials more than anything else. This has been helpful because I never want our tools and resources to be a burden. I try to remind our mentors that what I give them is a safety net and outline. I want them to dig deep into their personal experience and use that to make our Catholic faith relevant.

Mentors who have served for a few years will usually critique the community. Unlike other ministries, our mentors are on their own. Each year I try to form community and bring them together. This has been a challenge partially due to the other responsibilities I have as a youth minister, but it's something we are working on. My goal is to have coaches who serve as an extension of my office. In the meantime, I want our mentors to connect with each other on a personal basis. I want our mentors to work together to provide a service opportunity for their candidates. Sometimes when mentors meet with their candidates about the Engage step, they'll meet with another group to drive home the point of community.

One of the reasons I love my mentors is because of their honesty. They share with me their frustrations and their successes. They help me figure out what we can do better and what needs to be addressed. Without their feedback I would be lost.

LOOK AT THE LARGER PICTURE

Traditionally people look at Confirmation like a graduation from religious education. When I first started in youth ministry this perception was a reality. Most if not all of our candidates stopped coming to our high school program, and many stopped coming to Mass.

When we started incorporating habits and later steps into our program, we decided to measure how many students continued to grow in their faith after Confirmation was over. While taking attendance at Mass isn't plausible, we started to measure how many candidates stayed in ministry and continued with small groups.

With every new group of candidates our retention rate increases. In fact, some areas of our church have grown during the Confirmation process. It's allowed us to evaluate whether we were really providing opportunities for candidates to grow in the church.

Each year we look at new ways to measure. We might seem a little obsessed, but we want to know whether we are succeeding. Our high school program Uprising has helped us do that. We're able to see if candidates continue on with small groups and ministry. We can determine whether new students are coming because someone who has gone through preparation invited them. We are even looking at our offertory and determining whether people are intentionally or randomly giving.

This is something new for us, but having a separate youth ministry program will help you determine whether your Confirmation preparation is effective. The more you can measure, the more you can know.

PAY ATTENTION TO CANDIDATE LETTERS TO YOUR BISHOP

Our archdiocese asks that each candidate write a letter to the bishop reflecting on their experience and what they learned. Originally I saw this step, like the candidates, as an obligation. Later, after I started reading the letters, I learned this was an opportunity. While you will get some candidates telling the bishop what they think he wants to hear, you'll see that some will share with him what they want him to hear.

The first time I received a letter with a little bit of criticism I thought I would maybe hold on to it and not pass it along to the bishop. I was worried that the letter would reflect poorly on me, and that wouldn't be good. But then it was clear that something wasn't right. If our process was a disappointment to this candidate, maybe there was something we could learn from it. That's when I started to read more of them and use them as a way of gauging whether we were moving in the right direction.

Over my tenure I've encouraged the candidates to be real, authentic, and critical in their letters. I've asked them to share what they've learned and what they don't know. I read all the letters, which gets harder the more the program grows, but then I send them all to the bishop. We've had conversations about the letters, and he's always thankful for the candidate's ability to be candid and authentic. In fact, every year he shares a few of them at the Confirmation ceremony.

The letters are a way of letting us know what's working because a candidate will share with us what's had the most impact. The more personal the letter, the more we realize this program has had a personal impact on the candidate. When a letter talks about a specific mentor, we are able to evaluate how that mentor is doing.

Last, we take these letters and measure them up against the essays each candidate writes at the beginning of the process. We are able to look at the language they use when describing what it means to be a disciple and compare it to what they say at the end of their journey.

Having your candidates write letters is important because it helps you measure their experience and it also reminds you that what you do matters. There are going to be times when you wonder whether what you do is worth it, and these letters help you through those doubts. On top of being a tool for evaluation, they help you recruit new mentors. The letters show potential mentors the impact they can have. These letters help us remind current mentors that what they do makes a difference.

I know Confirmation preparation is a journey filled with struggles. After all, we are all growing disciples. We are all trying to figure out what God is calling us to do and how he wants us to do it. There will always be frustration when it comes to sacramental preparation, and that's because you are dealing with lives.

There is so much that I still have to learn when it comes to Confirmation. Each year I face doubts where I'm wondering whether what I do is worth it. It's those nights when I just want to scream on the way home, hide under the covers, and consider a new career. Preparing disciples to go into the world and set it on fire is part of a battle. I'm reminded each year at Mass that this is worth it. I believe there is a moment where each candidate, whether they openly went through the process or not, is witnessing the Spirit. You see the smile on their faces as the bishop anoints them, and it's a reminder that God is good all the time.

I don't want you to lose hope. The journey to fixing your Confirmation program will take time, but it is possible. Early on when I started in youth ministry I was frustrated, angry, and filled with despair. I would wonder, *What's the point?* and, *Is this really worth my time and energy?* And then each year as we made adjustments, I began to see God's fruit. I began to see teenagers approach Confirmation with excitement. Parents were excited to have their second and third child go through the program. Turnover decreased in our high school program, and the next generation's presence increased throughout the parish.

No matter how broken your program is, there is hope because you are doing God's work. Trust in him, and he will bless you continuously. I do believe your parish can fix Confirmation preparation; you just need to believe it too. Commit to one another and to the burden God has placed in your life. That burden at times will be heavy, but the work that you are putting into the process is worth it. It's changing lives.

APPENDIX A
CHURCH OF THE NATIVITY'S 2015–2016 CONFIRMATION APPLICATION

I: PERSONAL INFO

Baptized name:_____

Street address:_____

City:_____ State/zip: _____

Candidate's cell phone:_____ DOB: _____

Candidate's e-mail: _____

Best Way to Get in Touch: ☐ Text ☐ Call ☐ E-mail

The complete sacrament record is compiled at the child's parish of Baptism. Please provide accurate information so a certificate of Confirmation can be forwarded promptly.

Date of Baptism (mm/dd/yyyy):_____

Candidate's church of Baptism: _____

Church street address: _____

City:_____ State/zip: _____

Father's name:_____ Mother's name: _____

Family phone: _____

Family e-mail: _____

Best way to contact parents:　□ Call　□ E-mail

If there is a parent that is a primary contact please indicate here:

_____

II: ESSAY

Student's Essay

Please answer one of the following questions in a five-hundred-word essay. Please attach the completed essay to this form. The essay's purpose is to help the Confirmation mentor get a better sense of where the candidate is starting this part of the faith journey. Please be honest; there is no perfect answer.

1. What type of Christian man or woman do you envision being in the future?
2. What steps do you need to take to get closer to God?

Parent's Essay

Please answer one of the following questions in five hundred words or more. Please attach the completed essay to this form. The purpose of this essay is to help the Confirmation mentor get a better sense as to where your intentions for this sacrament meet those of your child's. Please be honest; there is no perfect answer.

1. How have you shared with your teen the importance of this sacrament?
2. What is the hope or vision you have for your child after he or she receives this sacrament?

III. SPONSOR AND NAME

My sponsor for Confirmation will be _____

Relation to candidate _____

My Confirmation name will be _____

Short explanation as to why I chose this name _____

_____

_____

_____

What are the requirements for a sponsor?

The Confirmation sponsor must be a confirmed, practicing Catholic. It cannot be a parent; however, the sponsor can be a grandparent or godparent. This should be someone the candidate trusts in seeking out faith advice and direction. While the popular choice is a family member or family friend, we also recommend small-group leaders and ministry leaders. This decision is up to the candidate.

What does a sponsor do during preparation?
A sponsor's role is very limited during the preparation. We ask that they do two things:

> Pray for the candidate.
> Check in on their preparation.

A sponsor's main duties will pick up where a mentor leaves off.

What are the requirements for a Confirmation name?
In order to manifest the close relationship of Confirmation to Baptism, the candidates, according to the longstanding custom of the Church, may retain their baptismal name. However, a special name may be chosen if desired, in which case it should be that of a recognized saint of the Church or a person from scripture (cf. canon 855).

IV: COMMITMENT FORM

Thank you for taking the time to discern a deeper commitment to your relationship with God. We hope that through this process you deepen your relationship with God, connect with other believers, discover your gifts and talents, grow in your faith, and see what an impact you can have on the church, the community, and the world.

By signing the bottom of this form I commit to

- deepening my relationship with God and the Church by fully participating in the preparation set forth by Church of the Nativity's student ministry, including the retreat provided by Church of the Nativity;
- meeting with a Confirmation mentor who will guide me through the resources, the curriculum, and steps that will help me in the development of spiritual habits;
- attending Mass on the weekends;
- taking the next step in my faith, whether that is participation in a season of small groups, ministry, or missions; and
- completing a final reflection letter to the bishop and the director of student ministry.

By signing this commitment form, I fully understand and agree to all the guidelines and procedures set forth by Church of the Nativity's student ministry program. I also understand that not fulfilling these commitments may delay the date on which I am confirmed.
Signature: _____ Date: _____

As a parent, I understand by signing this commitment form that I agree with and fully understand all the guidelines and procedures set forth by Church of the Nativity's student ministry program. I also understand that if my child does not fulfill each commitment, the date on which he or she is confirmed might be delayed.
Parent's signature: _____ Date: _____
Parent's signature: _____ Date: _____
At least one parent must sign this commitment.

APPENDIX B
NEXT STEPS: SERVE

DISCOVERING YOUR GPS: GPS PROFILE

We want the candidates to discover that God has created them for a unique purpose, with unique gifts and unique passions. We do this in something we call **GPS**. The goal of this exercise is to help them

1. discover their **G**ifts and abilities;
2. explore their **P**assion; and
3. look at their own sense of **S**elf, or their personality profile.

We hope the knowledge of their GPS will help guide candidates toward serving others throughout their lives.

Start by guiding the candidates through the next three parts to discover their GPS. This process is meant to help students discern the unique gifts, passions, and personality that God has given them.

PART I: GIFTS

Read the following to the student:

> We all have some skill. We're good at certain things from jumping rope to needlework to fixing appliances to delivering speeches. But when skill meets God—when skills collide with our God-given abilities—we have a true gift.

The candidates might know their gifts and abilities already, or these may be something they've never thought of. Help them brainstorm their gifts or abilities using the list provided. But before you show them the list, have them consider three responses they may have when they see each ability:

1. Love It! You can't imagine life without these activities; they make your day incredible. If you had the opportunity to make this your career, you would.
2. Like It! You enjoy them, but you don't need them to survive or be happy; you basically can take them or leave them.
3. Live Without It! You see these actions and you are like, "Forget about it." They leave you exhausted.

Read the following to the student:

> At Baptism God gave each of us a spiritual gift. A spiritual gift comes from God as part of your personal identity, and it's a gift to use your whole, entire life—not just when you're older or richer but now and always. God gives out these gifts personally, one by one.

Say: Combining what you now know about your gifts and abilities, name three spiritual gifts that you have (students can write these on their "Candidate Notes" page).

1.
2.
3.

Say: Now take some time with the following questions to reflect on your spiritual gifts:

1. Are other people helped when I use my gift?
2. Is God honored when I use my gift?
3. Do I feel fulfilled and used by God when I use my gift?

If the candidate feels the answer is no, tell them not to worry; they may have never viewed their gifts as spiritual. Have the candidate take another look at the list or think of other gifts and share the reason they may have been given these gifts and how they can use them.

LIST OF ABILITIES AND GIFTS

This is by no means an exhaustive list of gifts and abilities, so feel free to add your own as you and the candidate see fit. You may need to explain a few of these in a little more detail to your candidate—for example, if a student thinks he or she has the gift of being a good friend or sharing good advice, we have listed "counseling" to describe that kind of gift.

Art	Evangelization	Mercy
Building	Faith	Motivating
Coaching	Giving	Negotiating
Competing	Hospitality	Organizing
Cooking	Intercession	Performing
Counseling	Knowledge	Planning
Creating	Landscaping	Researching
Decorating	Leadership	Service
Designing	Learning	Skilled Craft
Directing	Managing	Teaching
Encouraging	Mentoring	Writing

PART II: PASSIONS

Read the following to the student:

> As you define your GPS you need to look into your heart. What do you really love to do? What brings you the most joy of all? If you "take delight in the Lord . . . he will give you your heart's desires." We know that's true because Jesus said it in the Gospel of John: "I came that you might have life in its fullest." God wants you to be happy!

Take some time with the student to discuss the following categories and their questions; have them record the answers in their handouts.

WHAT DO YOU REALLY LOVE DOING?

1. What do you really enjoy doing?
2. What thoughts fill your daydreams?
3. What motivates you to want to get off the couch?

Given your answers to these questions, how might God use what you love doing to help you serve others?

WHOM DO YOU LOVE SERVING?

1. Who has God brought into your life for a specific purpose?
2. What peer groups do you feel led to serve?
3. How could you serve others in a way that might allow you to use your spiritual gifts?
4. Are there other types of people you might enjoy serving? If so, who?

WHAT CAUSE WOULD YOU LOVE TO HELP CONQUER?

1. What issues makes your heart beat faster?
2. Where could you make the greatest impact for God?
3. If time were not a concern, how would you like to serve God?

Considering what they discovered in the last two sections, have the candidate write down what gifts/activities he or she cannot live without.

PART III: SELF

Read the following to the student:

Without a doubt, your personality is just as God intended. Sometimes we wish we were more like other people, but the honest truth is, your personality is perfect. God designed it. Personality is how you encounter life and how you express it. It's how you naturally respond to situations and circumstances. Whether you're reserved or outgoing, whether you prefer to plan out your day or have no definite schedule at all, whether you think or feel your way through decisions, your personality was created by God just the way God wanted you to be.

Before starting the next step, discuss the following:

- How do you typically relate to other people?
- How do you respond to opportunities, crises, invitations, or changes?

Have the candidate discern his or her personality with the following exercise. (Note: this is not a scientific process. It's just to get their thoughts flowing.)

Responding to Others

Circle one capitalized term in each numbered category below and then mark True or False for each statement that follows to confirm your decisions.

1. Around others I am more: RESERVED or OUTGOING (circle one)
Mark T or F next to the following statements:
    _____ I find ways to be part of the crowd.
    _____ I build deep relationships with a few friends, not large numbers of people.
    _____ I start conversations with people I don't know.
    _____ I avoid being part of a large group.

2. My decisions are based more on: FACTS/THINKING or FEELINGS (circle one)
Mark T or F next to the following statements:

_____ I feel free to share my feelings with people I've just met.

_____ I withhold my thoughts and feelings from others at certain times.

_____ I seek opportunities to share my life with others.

_____ I hold back so only a few close friends can truly know me.

3. In my relationships I tend to be more: COOPERATIVE or COMPETITIVE (circle one)

Mark T or F next to the following statements:

_____ I focus on making sure people feel comfortable when I'm around them.

_____ I find importance in achievements.

_____ I look for ways to make others content.

_____ I embrace conflict and enjoy winning.

Responding to Opportunities

1. I tend to be more: HIGH RISK or LOW RISK (circle one)

Mark T or F next to the following statements:

_____ I avoid radical changes.

_____ I enjoy chaotic environments.

_____ I excel when risk is very low.

_____ I get motivated when I have the chance to overcome big obstacles.

2. I am drawn more to: PEOPLE or PROJECTS (circle one)

Mark T or F next to the following statements:

_____ I embrace opportunities to work with other people directly.

_____ I look for ways to complete projects.

_____ I enjoy being involved in many projects at once.

_____ I find more fulfillment when I can work with someone one-on-one or in a small group.

3. I like to: FOLLOW or LEAD (circle one)

Mark T or F next to the following statements:

_____ I often find myself leading others.

_____ I feel comfortable when I can follow someone else.

_____ I determine the direction for groups I'm part of.
_____ I experience fulfillment when I help others succeed.

4. I enjoy: BEING ON A TEAM or FLYING SOLO (circle one)
Mark T or F next to the following statements:
_____ I enjoy being part of a team or group.
_____ I look for opportunities that allow me to work by myself.
_____ I become energized by being around others.
_____ I work most effectively when I'm alone.

5. I am all about: ROUTINE or VARIETY (circle one)
Mark T or F next to the following statements:
_____ I tend to be involved in many projects at one time.
_____ I prefer completing one project before starting another.
_____ I enjoy being responsible for a lot of tasks at the same time.
_____ I become overwhelmed with constant change.

Discuss with the candidate: How does your personality match up with the gifts you have and with your passions? What have you learned about yourself during this GPS process?

BIBLIOGRAPHY

Archdiocese of Baltimore. *Seal of the Spirit*. Baltimore: Keeler, Cardinal William, March 20, 2000. http://www.archbalt.org/youth-young-adult/youth-programs/upload/The-Seal-of-the-Spirit.pdf.

Brown, Chris. "3 Things the Bible Says About Money." *Stewardship*, May 21, 2015. http://www.stewardship.com/.

Canon Law Society of America. *Code of Canon Law: Latin–English Edition*. Vatican City: Libreria Editrice Vaticana, 1983.

Catechism of the Catholic Church: Revised in Accordance with the Official Latin Text Promulgated by Pope John Paul II. Vatican City: Libreria Editrice Vaticana, 1997.

Francis. "*Evangelii Gaudium*: Encyclical Letter, Francis." Vatican: The Holy See, November 24, 2013. http://w2.vatican.va/.

"Saint Isidore of Seville." CatholicSaints.Info. http://catholicsaints.info/saint-isidore-of-seville/.

"Saint Margaret Mary Alocoque." Saintsquotes.blogspot.com. http://saintquotes.blogspot.com/2009/05/prayer.html.

Stanley, Andy. *7 Practices of Effective Ministry*. Colorado Springs, CO: Multnomah Books, 2004.

White, Michael, and Tom Corcoran. *Rebuilt: Awakening the Faithful, Reaching the Lost, and Making Church Matter*. Notre Dame, IN: Ave Maria Press, 2013.

CHRISTOPHER WESLEY is a youth ministry coach and consultant with Marathon Youth Ministry (christopherwesley.org). He served as the director of student ministry at Church of the Nativity in Timonium, Maryland, for more than twelve years. He also serves as the president of the unCUFFed Ministries Board of Directors in Baltimore, Maryland. The author of *Rebuilding Youth Ministry*, Wesley writes content for downloadyouthministry.com.

Wesley has a bachelor's degree in communication arts, electronic media, from Xavier University in Cincinnati, Ohio. A native of Mountain Lakes, New Jersey, Wesley has lived in Tokyo; Hong Kong; Auckland, New Zealand; Cincinnati, Ohio; and Baltimore. He and his wife, Katherine, have two sons and live in Pikesville, Maryland.